SAINTS AND SOCIETY

SAINTS AND SOCIETY

*The Social Impact of
Eighteenth Century English Revivals
and Its Contemporary Relevance*

By
EARLE E. CAIRNS
*Chairman of the Department of History
and Political Science*
Wheaton College

WIPF & STOCK · Eugene, Oregon

Wipf and Stock Publishers
199 W 8th Ave, Suite 3
Eugene, OR 97401

Saints and Society
The Social Impact of Eighteenth Century English Revivals
and Its Contemporary Relevance
By Cairns, Earle E.
Softcover ISBN-13: 978-1-6667-1977-2
Hardcover ISBN-13: 978-1-6667-1978-9
eBook ISBN-13: 978-1-6667-1979-6
Publication date 4/30/2021
Previously published by Moody Press, 1960

This edition is a scanned facsimile of
the original edition published in 1960.

To
My Mother

CONTENTS

FOREWORD 9
PREFACE 11
I. THE SETTING FOR EVANGELICAL
   REFORM 1648-1789 17
     I. POLITICAL CONDITIONS 17
    II. ECONOMIC TRENDS 20
   III. SOCIAL DEVELOPMENTS 21
   IV. THE INTELLECTUAL CLIMATE OF OPINON. 24
    V. THE LITERARY WORLD 25
   VI. RELIGIOUS CONDITIONS 26
II. THE SOURCES OF EVANGELICAL
   REFORM 29
     I. THE WESLEYAN REVIVAL 30
       A. GEORGE WHITEFIELD 30
       B. THE WESLEYS 33
    II. THE EVANGELICAL REVIVAL 36
III. THE SCOPE OF EVANGELICAL
   REFORM..................................... 44
     I. SPIRITUAL AND PHYSICAL FREEDOM
       FOR COLORED PEOPLES 44
       A. SPIRITUAL MEASURES FOR FREEING COLORED MEN. 44
       B. FREEING COLORED MEN FROM PHYSICAL SLAVERY. 56
         1. *Abolition of Slavery in England and Colonization of Ex-slaves in Sierra Leone 1772-1807* 61
         2. *The Abolition and Suppression of the European Slave Trade 1787-1807*........... 66
         3. *The Amelioration of Slavery 1808-1823*..... 76
         4. *Abolition of Slavery in the British Empire 1823-1833* 77
         5. *The Protection of Colored People after 1834*. 86
         6. *Treaty States and Protectorates*............ 94
    II. SPIRITUAL AND PHYSICAL FREEDOM FOR
       THE WORKERS OF ENGLAND............102

    A. FREEDOM FOR THE SOULS AND MINDS OF
       WORKING ENGLISHMEN 102
    B. PHYSICAL FREEDOM FOR ENGLISHMEN 106
       1. Prison Reform 106
       2. The Emancipation of the Insane........... 108
       3. The Emancipation of the Workers of
          England 111

IV. THE SPIRIT OF EVANGELICAL REFORM 120
   I. THE BASIS OF WESLEY'S SOCIAL THOUGHT . 120
   II. THE SPIRIT OF WILBERFORCE'S
      SOCIAL ACTIVITY 123
   III. THE SPIRIT OF SHAFTESBURY'S SERVICE
      TO THE WORKERS OF ENGLAND........ 128

V. SAINTS AND SOCIETY IN THE TWENTIETH CENTURY 133
   I. THE SPIRIT OF EVANGELICAL
      SOCIAL ACTIVITY 139
      A. FAITH 140
      B. LOVE 143
      C. HOPE 146
   II. THE STRATEGY OF EVANGELICAL
      SOCIAL ACTIVITY 148
      A. SECURING THE FACTS 148
      B. TECHNIQUES TO CREATE CHRISTIAN PUBLIC
         OPINION 151
      C. METHODS TO OBTAIN ACTION 153
   III. THE SCOPE OF EVANGELICAL
      SOCIAL ACTIVITY 155
      A. THE FAMILY 156
      B. THE CHURCH 160
      C. SOCIETAL RELATIONSHIPS 162
        1. Political Responsibilities 162
        2. Economic Responsibilities 170
        3. Social Responsibilities 175

BIBLIOGRAPHY 181
INDEX 189

FOREWORD

THE GOSPEL is indeed the power of God to salvation to every believer. To experience forgiveness of sins and assurance of acceptance with God is a profound, transforming experience, but it is not an end in itself. The divine power that redeems the individual places within him the dynamic to reach others with the same message and to arrest anti-Christian social forces in the social order.

Salvation is not only an emotional experience for the individual Christian, it extends to every area of his life and to the society in which he moves. As the Saviour Himself faced the disease and depravity of His day, and brought transformation to many, even so the Christian by his words and his deeds challenges the wrong and seeks to change conditions for the better.

The Gospel has its social implications. The human heart is not set free from the bondage and burden of sin by an improvement in environment, but life should be better for all because there are vibrant and victorious Christians in the community. Believers in Christ are to be "the salt of the earth," with the wholesome and helpful effect of that substance.

The religious impact of the revivals that swept through Britain and the American colonies under the Wesleys, Whitefield and others in the middle of the eighteenth century has been well told. But the social impact thereof has not received the same understanding. Professor Cairns traces the great changes in social conditions to the evangelical awakenings and portrays clearly the implications of the Gospel to the social order. It is a challenging account of change made by men and women who themselves were changed by the power of the gospel.

V. RAYMOND EDMAN
President, Wheaton College

PREFACE

THE RELATIONSHIP of the Christian to the social order has always been of deep personal concern to Christians. This problem has come into sharp focus in the twentieth century in the tension which exists in many lands between the interests of the individual and those of the group. The liberal ideal of the nineteenth century, which emphasized freedom for the individual in his political, economic, intellectual, social, religious and aesthetic life, has been challenged by a corporate or totalitarian view of life in which the interests of the state have priority over those of the individual. The existence of the state becomes an end to which the interests of the individual as a means must be sacrificed. Because of this challenge to the sacredness of human personality and the dignity of the individual, Evangelicals must rethink the question of the role of the individual in every area of social life in order that the Christian ethic may be applied to social situations.

A world divided between two views of life confronts us. The Communist view denies that the individual, because he is a potential or actual son of God by faith in Christ, has dignity, whereas the western world still asserts this ideal. This international ideological division of the world has been complicated since World War II by the power vacuums arising from the total defeat of Germany and Japan and the decline of the old imperial powers. This decline has been accompanied by the rise of Afro-Asian nationalism with its insistent and often rebellious demand for independence. Communist leaders, unhampered by ethical considerations or the desire for peace, have exploited this situation by moving into areas of political vacuum or by stirring up native peoples against their former colonial masters.

This division is made even more dangerous by technological developments which have shrunk both space and time and which have placed what seem to be weapons for absolute destruction in the hands of man. Such tension and crisis put upon the Christian the insistent responsibility to rethink his role in society in the light of history and, above all, the Bible.

The author has studied and thought about the problem of the relation of the saint to society for over twenty years. Study as an undergraduate of the nineteenth century social reforms in England achieved by the Evangelicals and the relationship between those reforms and the Methodist and evangelical revivals of the eighteenth century created a deep interest in this field. Both his thesis for the master's degree and his doctoral dissertation were devoted to a study of the impact of revival upon the work of missionaries in Africa in exploration, road-building, trade, education, philology and even empire-building as a means of bringing the natives under the protection of governments with more humane colonial policies. It was discovered that these by-products of missionary activity were used as means to the end—the conversion of the soul.

Supervision in the graduate school of Wheaton College of a thesis by Robert Loveless on the social views of Walter Rauschenbusch and of another by John Wiens on the Biblical motives inspiring John Wesley, William Wilberforce and Lord Shaftesbury in their work of social reform further developed this interest. Thomas Askew kindly helped in the development of this book by the careful collection of relevant bibliography. The invitation to present the Lyman Stewart Memorial Lectures in Talbot Seminary in Los Angeles in January, 1957, provided the impetus to continue research in the original documents over a two-year period.

Preface 13

The writer is indebted to several who have carefully read and constructively criticized this work in manuscript form. Matthew S. Evans made many constructive stylistic suggestions. The careful reading by the author's wife, by V. Raymond Edman, president of Wheaton College, by Gordon Jaeck and Lamberta Voget, colleagues on the faculty, and by Frank Farrell, of the editorial staff of *Christianity Today,* enabled the writer to improve the presentation. The publication of the gist of this work in the September 14, 1959, issue of *Christianity Today,* under the title, "Saints and the Social Order," was an added kindness of the editors. Typing of the manuscript by Patricia LaBorde and checking by other students have contributed much to the completed work.

Several approaches have been used by those studying Christian social reform in England and the relation of the Christian to his society. Writers dominated by the rationalistic climate of opinion of the past either minimize the work of Christian reformers or ridicule it as impractical and claim that they were blind to other problems of importance. For instance, Charles Dickens, in his novel, *Bleak House,* pictures missionaries as top-hatted, frock-coated, umbrella in hand, Bible-carrying individuals who were quite impractical. Their supporters at home are satirized in the brilliant literary sketch of Mrs. Jellyby, who is more interested in the cultivation of the coffee berry and the natives of "Borrioboola-Gha on the left bank of the Niger" than in her neglected family, at times famished for food as well as affection.

Another group treats the Evangelicals fairly by giving them credit for humane social changes, but errs in ascribing their reforms to their belief in the dogma of the fatherhood of God and the brotherhood of man. Paul Knaplund in his excellent book, *James Stephen and the Colonial System 1814-1847* (Madison, Wis.: University of Wisconsin Press, 1953), asserts that James Stephen's fight against slavery and the illtreatment of the aborigines in British colonies was the result of his thought on the fatherhood of God and the brotherhood of man (p. 15). Earnest M. Howse's fine little book, *Saints in Politics* (Toronto, Can.: University of Toronto Press, 1952), gives an excellent and sympathetic presentation of the work of the Evangelicals but concludes that their reforms were inspired by the religious dogma of the fatherhood of God and the brotherhood of man (p. viii). It seems to the author that these men were reading their theological presuppositions into the thinking of the evangelicals.

Still others exhibit better spiritual perception in finding the motive of evangelical social reforms in the belief in salvation by faith through Christ's work on the cross and the consequent value of the human personality. They err, however, in setting such reforms in a postmillennial framework which these men were supposed to hold. J. W. Bready, in his splendid biography of Shaftesbury, holds more tenaciously than the facts warrant to the idea that men were saved to save society. Instead, Shaftesbury really looked to the Second Coming of Christ as the final solution to the ills of society.

The author's studies show the need for an objective historical study based upon primary documents which reveal the Biblical and evangelical motivation of these Christian social reformers. Evangelicals have given too little consideration to this matter from an empirical and historical viewpoint. Carl F. H. Henry has presented an interesting and useful theological and philosophical approach to the problem in *The Uneasy Conscience of Modern Fundamentalism* (Grand Rapids, Mich.: Wm. B. Eerdman's Publishing Co., 1947), but he did not discuss the matter from an historical viewpoint because his aim was to arouse evangelicals to consider the social implications of the gospel. Sympathetic yet objective study of the reforms and the writings of the reformers and other primary sources will throw light upon the problem which has vexed the Church since its inception—the relation of the Christian to his social context. Sources are not usually cited but reference to the bibliography will make them accessible to those interested in further study in this field.

It is the hope and prayer of the author that this discussion of the social impact of revivalism in England will alert Evangelicals to the responsibility which they have as citizens of earth as well as of Heaven. If some are made aware that they have a horizontal orientation of love in action toward their fellows as well as a vertical orientation of faith toward God for personal salvation, the author will be satisfied. If the Evangelical believes in the Second Advent of Christ, participation in social change should lead neither to a blithe optimism that social reform will create Utopia nor to a paralyzing despair concerning a perishing temporary world in which the Christian mistakenly thinks that his only responsibility is to prepare his own soul for the coming of Christ. Instead the Christian will realize that his task is to "occupy" socially as well as personally until the Lord does come.

E. E. CAIRNS
Wheaton, Illinois

March, 1960

Chapter I

THE SETTING FOR EVANGELICAL REFORM IN ENGLAND
1648-1789

ALTHOUGH THE ROOTS of modern civilization may be found in the period of the Renaissance between 1350 and 1648, the greatest development of modern European civilization (which is also that of the United States) took place during the following century and a half. This age had its beginning in 1648 with the Treaty of Westphalia, which marked the development of the modern nation-state system, and came to an end in 1789 with the beginning of the French Revolution. An understanding of this era is essential in order to know the background of and the need for desirable social reforms in the nineteenth century. Most of these reforms were to come from the inspiration of the great revivals which occurred during what modern historians usually call the Age of Reason. If the eighteenth century may be characterized as the Age of Reason, the nineteenth century may be looked upon as the Age of Reform.

I. POLITICAL CONDITIONS

During this period the English government changed from an absolute divine right monarchy to one based upon the natural law theory of John Locke. The rest of Europe held either to an absolute divine right monarchy or to an enlightened absolutism in which the ruler was a benevolent despot whose enlightened and superior mind would guide him to do what was best for his people. Frederick the Great of Prussia, Catherine II of Russia and Louis XIV of France followed this ideal. The future, in some countries at least, was to rest with governments based upon the sovereignty of the people. This type appeared in England after the fall of the Stuarts during the Glorious, or Bloodless, Revolution of 1688. Until the political reforms of the nineteenth century, England was governed by a constitutional monarch who reigned, while Parliament, dominated by an aristocracy, ruled the land in the interests of that small segment of the popuuation which alone had the right to vote.

John Locke (1632-1704), in his *Two Treatises of Government,* published in 1690, provided both the rationalization for the revolution of 1688 and the political theory to justify control of the country by the people, even if it were only the upper class segment of the population. He argued that prior to organized government man enjoyed certain natural rights, such as life, liberty and property, but because the strong oppressed the weak, men entered into a social contract or compact to set up a government with the task of protecting these natural rights. If the rulers violated the natural rights of the people, they had the right to revolt and to create a new government. The American Declaration of Independence was another classic expression of Locke's political philosophy.

Rousseau in 1762 published his *Social Contract* which also emphasized the sovereignty of the people. This sovereignty, according to him, expressed itself in the general will which would be made known by a majority vote. He did not, however, have any protection for the rights of the minority who must be coerced into an acceptance of the general will. The slogan of liberty, equality and fraternity of the French Revolution was a practical expression of this philosophy.

The Setting for Evangelical Reform in England 19

It will be noticed that the natural rights theory of the English, American and French Revolutions had little to say about the fact that absolute sovereignty belongs to God and that government comes from God to whom both ruler and ruled are responsible. This may help to explain the sorry plight of English government by the end of the French Revolution. The chief executive, George III, would have been an excellent farmer had he been free to follow his interests, but he made a poor ruler.

His son, the Prince of Wales, who became George IV in 1820, was far from being an ideal ruler. He married Caroline of Brunswick from whom he separated after the birth of their child. He then lived with a succession of feminine favorites, selected from the court. The early part of his reign was marked by the scandal in which Caroline claimed her right to be Queen of England. This immoral ruler, who aspired to be an Adonis, was somewhat cowardly and effeminate.

His brothers were little better. The Duke of Kent, although a religious man, brought about a mutiny in the army at Gibraltar by his strict discipline. The Duke of York had a mistress who, with his full knowledge and consent, carried on a profitable trade in the sale of commissions in the armed services.

Because administrators under these men derived most of their income from fees in addition to their salaries, much corruption characterized administration. Each department had a separate treasury, and on more than one occasion the head of a department kept money inactive and collected the interest on it for himself. Others had sinecures—jobs which paid well but for which they did no work or used a poorly paid substitute to do the work. Many received pensions to which they had no legal right.

The political and moral failure of the executive was matched by that of the legislature. Lord Chesterfield was laughed at when he tried to buy a seat in the House of Commons for his son at the low price of £2,500. The price of a seat rose from £1,000 to £5,000 in the early part of the eighteenth century. Seats in Parliament were openly advertised for sale in *The Times* of London. Walpole, when he was the leader of the cabinet in the reign of George I, said of the members of Parliament that each one had his price and could be bribed into doing what he wanted. Bribery was facilitated by the existence of pocket boroughs and rotten boroughs. The former were districts where the owner of the area controlled the vote, and the latter were districts which had few or no voters. Old Sarum with no buildings or people in it was represented in Parliament by a member chosen by the owner. Camelford borough, owned by the Duke of Bedford, had nine electors who voted as the Duke desired because he owned their homes. The Duke sold his borough in 1812 for £32,000. About 1800 the election of the 560 members of the House of Commons was in the hands of approximately 1,500 men.

Prime Minister Walpole controlled George II by getting him an annual grant of £100,000 and controlled George's wife by promising her more than his rival for control of the cabinet could promise. It was his settled policy to keep a majority in the House of Commons by the clever use of patronage. He gave his sons sinecures valued at £15,000 per year, and when he realized that he could not remain in power much longer, he secured for himself a pension worth £4,000 and the title of Earl of Oxford. Such was the state of the executive and the legislative branches of government during the eighteenth and early nineteenth centuries.

II. ECONOMIC TRENDS

The economic outlook of the period was also hostile to the spirit of reform. Mercantilistic theory, which originated in the seventeenth century, emphasized the need for self-sufficiency of the state through a favorable trade balance. It also

The Setting for Evangelical Reform in England 21

advocated the exploitation of the colonies in order to supplement the economy of the mother country. These ideas led to the detailed regimentation and regulation of the economic life of the state irrespective of the needs of the people as individuals. Reform could not be allowed to interfere with the economic interests of the state.

Adam Smith attacked this system in the *Wealth of Nations,* published in 1776. He argued that business should be left completely free from government control. Natural laws of supply and demand, competition and enlightened self-interest would lead the businessman to seek his own self-interest and to act so that society would have the benefit. Unfortunately, Adam Smith, optimistically holding to fixed natural economic laws, did not realize that sin would promote greed which would result in monopoly. Governments, said Smith, should not interfere with the conduct of business. Government functions only for the protection of contracts and property. It could levy necessary taxes to carry out these duties. This view, which was to replace mercantilism in the nineteenth century, was no more friendly to reform than mercantilism had been. Wilberforce's attempts to help the slaves and Shaftesbury's efforts on behalf of the workers of England were often condemned as invasions of the rights of private property. Freedom was the prerogative of the owners of factories and fields but was not for the workers in those factories or fields.

III. SOCIAL DEVELOPMENTS

Social conditions in England during the eighteenth and nineteenth centuries cried out for the efforts of social reformers. In the late eighteenth century one might be hanged for commiting any one of about 160 crimes. In the early nineteenth century the death penalty could be invoked for any one of more than 200 crimes. Snaring a rabbit or taking over one shilling from another's pocket might bring the death penalty. In 1732, seventy were sentenced to death in Old Bailey, one of the courts. Executions of more than a dozen people at Tyburn every six weeks were popularly described as "Hanging Shows" to which one might take the whole family as to a fair. People paid for seats around the gallows where they could callously watch the death struggles of the hanged man. Jailers were not paid salaries but lived by fees which they extracted from their prisoners or their families. Hence jails were often filthy places. The severity of punishment did not stop crime, because the certainty of punishment was nullified by juries who often refused to give the death penalty for what were really misdemeanors rather than crimes.

Popular sports of the time illustrate this same callousness toward life. An advertisement in a London paper in the decade of Wesley's conversion (1738) spoke of the rare sport to be provided for the patrons by a mad bull dressed in fireworks, a cat tied to its tail, a dog dressed in fireworks and a bear to be let loose at the same time. Cockfights with the spurs and beaks of the cocks sharpened provided a bloody occasion for gamblers betting on their favorites. Bear-and-badger-baiting with dogs were common. Boxing and other sports were conducted under brutal conditions with little protection for the performers. Even women fought with each other in the most brutal of wrestling and boxing bouts.

Drunkenness was a national habit of all classes. The 527,000 gallons of distilled spirits consumed in 1684 rose to two million gallons in 1714 and to eleven million gallons at the peak of production in 1750. In 1750 over 500 of the 2,000 houses in St. Giles in London were gin shops. Patronage was solicited by ads such as "Drunk for 1d; Dead Drunk, 2d; Free Straw." Some signs added the words "Clean Straw for Nothing" upon which one might sleep off the effects of the gin. Unfortunately, the workers gave up their milder ale for the cheaper and more potent gin which threatened their

The Setting for Evangelical Reform in England 23

sanity if used too long and heavily. The London death rate rose to one in twenty at times between 1720 and 1750 when gin was freely consumed, but dropped when a high tax was placed on distilled spirits in 1751. The Wesleyan revival, which won many workers to Christ and sobriety after 1739, was also an important factor in the more favorable statistics after 1750.

Such drunkenness was not confined to the workers. More than once the House of Commons had to adjourn early because the "honourable members" were too drunk to carry on public business. Walpole is said on good authority to have urged his son Robert to drink twice to his once so that the son would not be sober enough to see his father drunk. An Anglican minister, who was rebuked by the Bishop of Chester, defended himself by the assertion that he was never drunk while on duty in the church service. The bishop's question as to when a clergyman was not on duty seemed to surprise him.

Gambling also became a national mania during the eighteenth century. The shares of the South Sea Company which was chartered in 1711 rose from a face value of £100 per share to £1,060 in 1720 before the break in value that year. People were able to recover only one-third of the face value of their stock through the efforts of Walpole. He had sold his shares just before the break at a great profit.

Individuals gambled at the gambling table as well as in stocks. Horace Walpole in 1770 claimed that losses of £10,000, £15,000, or even £20,000 by young men were not uncommon losses for one evening at the table. Lord Stavordale, who lost £11,000, won it back in one hand. Charles James Fox owed £100,000 for gambling debts by the time he was twenty-four. Betting at horse racing, cockfighting and many other sports was common.

The social conditions which have been described provide the background for revival. One can but marvel at the grace of God displayed in revival in the late eighteenth century and social reform in the nineteenth century in view of these conditions.

IV. THE INTELLECTUAL CLIMATE OF OPINION

Political, economic and social trends become more understandable in the light of intellectual conditions in eighteenth century England. It was pre-eminently an age of reason. Francis Bacon had extolled the virtues of the inductive method, in which facts are observed in order to arrive at general principles. By this method man was to conquer nature. Locke's *Essay Concerning Human Understanding* emphasized the idea that human senses are the basic source of knowledge. Isaac Newton's discoveries in the field of physics seemed to unify all the data of the physical sciences, and he developed the concept of a universe run according to natural laws. As a result the world came to be looked upon as a machine which God had created and left to operate under natural law. God was thus an absentee landlord whose estate ran itself. This idea of natural laws in the realm of physics was carried over into economics by Adam Smith, into politics by Rousseau and Montesquieu, and even into religion by the Deists. Presumably God became unnecessary in such a world and was retired to its fringes.

Rationalistic philosophers, such as Descartes, proclaimed the power of reason in the acquisition of knowledge. With the emphasis on the scientific method and the power of man's unaided reason to obtain truth, reason replaced revelation as the source of authority. Condorcet in the late eighteenth century argued that man was not a sinner but was perfectible and could make progress towards a future Utopia by his own unaided efforts. Such men were optimistic that secular advance would be enough to create the perfect society. This belief in the goodness and perfectibility of man led Rousseau to proclaim in his *Émile* that there was no such thing as original sin. The individual was free to perfect himself and his society.

It is small wonder then that Alexander Pope in his *Essay on Man* should have found the main revelation of God in nature. He wrote that man should not presume to "scan" God because the proper study to which men should commit themselves was "man" in his various activities. Love of God and love of man in this rationalistic sense is, he concluded, the end of all activity.

V. THE LITERARY WORLD

With the exception of Pope, the major literary effort of the Age of Reason was prose. This literary form seemed better fitted than poetry to an age which believed that reason and the scientific method were man's greatest aids in the advancement of learning. This is the era in which the novel was born and in which the English dictionary was compiled by Samuel Johnson. Jonathan Swift's rational, biting wit pictured the oppression of the Irish by absentee landlords in his *A Modest Proposal*. In it he suggested that the English landlords might as well import Irish children to England for meat and retain the Irish parents to produce more children for the meat market because they had taken everything else away from them. He also satirized English society in *Gulliver's Travels*.

The emphasis on rationalism led to the beliefs that form was more important than content and that the study of the classical literature of Greece was an important asset to the development of good literary form. The Biblically oriented literature of Milton and Bunyan gave way to prose literature which seemed to suit the rationalism and loose morality of the age.

VI. RELIGIOUS CONDITIONS

The skepticism and rationalism of the upper classes was an attempt partly to escape the restraints of Christian morality and partly to be considered enlightened. Religion was supported as a means to keep the lower classes in order. Reason and morality were the essentials of a religion which had no spiritual dynamic. Any emotional expression of religious belief was classed as "enthusiasm" of which no well-bred person would be guilty. Deism seemed to them to be the most suitable religious expression of man's deepest thoughts concerning his origin, present duty and future destiny.

Lord Herbert of Cherbury gave the first expression to the dogmas of Deism in 1624. He took the existence of God as the first of his theological postulates. Christ was but a man who best expressed the ethical will of this God. Prayer and miracle were alike valueless because this God was bound by natural laws which He could not break to answer prayer even if He were interested in so doing. Man was to live ethically. The Bible thus became a guidebook for ethics rather than a revelation of the will of God. Man should live ethically in view of the fact that he was immortal and would face either retribution or happiness in a future world. These views seemed to be reinforced by the discovery that other religions of man, such as those in the Far East, had similar principles. Thus it was assumed that there was a natural religion of reason with natural ethical laws. In this manner the natural laws and mechanistic interpretation of nature were carried over into religion. This reduced religion to an empty, ethical system which lacked the spiritual dynamic that was needed to enable man to live up to the ethical standards of reason.

With such a view becoming popular among the clergy as well as the upper classes, it is not strange that the clergy of the Established Church should have been so deficient in their duty. They were not immoral but were interested in the ad-

The Setting for Evangelical Reform in England 27

vancement of their own fortunes. Of 10,000 positions in the Church of England shortly after 1700, nearly 6,000 paid under £50 a year and 1,200 paid under £20 a year. It was hard to get men to staff these poorly paid positions. In 1809, 7,358 of 11,194 clergymen did not reside in their parishes, although they collected the salaries. The higher clergy fared better. The Archbishop of Canterbury received £7,000 a year while the Archbishop of York earned £4,500 a year. The Bishop of Durham was given £6,000 a year. John Potter, while he was Archbishop of Canterbury between 1737 and 1747, amassed a fortune of £90,000. George III had to advise Cornwallis, then Archbishop of Canterbury, that he must stop his scandalous "routs and feasts" at Lambeth, the episcopal palace, or the king would be forced to take harsher measures. One clergyman deliberately bet Lady Yarmouth £5,000 that he would not become a bishop. She took up the bet and pulled the proper strings so that she won her £5,000, but the clergyman was not surprised to receive an appointment as a bishop.

Preaching had an ethical and class emphasis. Respect for the upper classes and loyalty to the king were notes regularly sounded in sermons. Late eighteenth century homilies on morals were characterized by Leslie Stephen as "dull, duller, and dullest." William Blackstone, the great lawyer, who went to hear every noted London clergyman in his day said that there was as much Christianity in the writings of Cicero as in their sermons and that one would be hard put to tell from the sermon whether the minister was a Confucianist, Mohammedan or Christian. The Bishop of Gloucester, writing against the Methodists, called talk of the new birth "mere enthusiasm or fanaticism."

Nonconformists were as dogmatically indifferent as their brethren in the state church. Many were Arian in their denial of the deity of Christ. Presbyterians more readily lapsed into Unitarianism than the Baptists. The Presbyterians, who constituted two-thirds of the Dissenters in 1715, were only one-twentieth in 1815. The existence of God, the necessity of virtue and immortality were about the only doctrines left to which many of the clergy of the state church and nonconformist groups held. It is little wonder the eighteenth century was ripe for revival.

The above conditions, which can be readily documented from contemporary literature, made revival and reform imperative if England were to continue on into the nineteenth century as an important nation. Her leadership in the nineteenth century was largely a result of the fact that she did have revival and that godly men sought to improve the sorry situation described in this chapter. They did this by successfully carrying out reforms which were inspired by their experience of salvation and guided by Biblical ethics.

Chapter II

THE SOURCES OF EVANGELICAL REFORM

EIGHTEENTH CENTURY ENGLAND was a land of political, social and economic privilege for the upper classes, but a nation where the workers in the town and country had to endure a position of social inferiority and economic injustice without any political expression of their miseries and without any means to redress them. The rationalistic religion of Deism dominated the thinking of the clergy and the upper class, and the people were left in brutish religious indifference until the Wesleyan revival. The rigid application of natural law to economics, as expressed in the writings of Adam Smith and Ricardo, made any political attempts at reform worthless because, according to these writers, natural economic laws could not be changed.

During the nineteenth century England became a land where each person was given the privileges of basic education, limited hours of labor, protection from dangerous machinery and better housing. Slaves were freed throughout British possessions, and the slave trade was virtually stopped. Missionary societies were engaged in the civilization as well as the conversion of the aborigines. The principle of trusteeship toward the native populations of the colonies was accepted by British public opinion as a moral responsibility.

This social transformation was due to an enlightened social

conscience, alert statesmen of principle and humane colonial legislators. These statesmen and legislators accepted their responsibilities as citizens because they had become Christians.

The social dynamic was mainly the result of revival after 1739. Social reform was not left to professional social workers or to sentimental crusaders. Such work was accepted as a calling of God by statesmen, such as Wilberforce and Shaftesbury. They had the backing of converted people whose Christianity was also expressed in political support of social change along Christian lines. It will be seen that all classes were affected by the earlier Wesleyan and the later evangelical revivals.

I. THE WESLEYAN REVIVAL

Despite the prevailing rationalism of the times, revival was a widespread phenomenon of the religious scene during the eighteenth century. The Methodist revival in England was paralleled by the Great Awakening in the thirteen colonies, and the two were linked by the preaching of Whitefield, who was a friend of such American religious leaders as Jonathan Edwards and Gilbert Tennent. It was this religious movement in England with its desire for social change, as well as its passion for the salvation of souls, which was the dynamic of social reform in nineteenth century England. Whitefield was its orator-prophet, John Wesley its able organizer and administrator, and Charles Wesley its song writer.

A. GEORGE WHITEFIELD

The evangelistic passion for souls and a zeal for social reform were closely united in George Whitefield (1714-1770). He brought new spiritual life into the Presbyterian and Congregational churches of England and created a Calvinistic Methodist church.

Whitefield, whose father died when George was only two years old, was the youngest of seven children of the owner of

The Sources of Evangelical Reform

the Bell Inn of Gloucester. His grammar school education, based on classical studies, developed his natural ability in speaking. He loved to read dramatic plays. After three years at the grammar school he was put to work in the inn. A quarrel with his sister-in-law, whose husband had taken over the inn, was solved by his going to Bristol where he began to read devotional material. Here, as he put it, he fell into "atheistical" company. He joined in sin and mocked at religion. One day he overheard friends speak well of him and became so ashamed of his hypocrisy that he made a moral resolve to do better.

When he found he could earn his way in college by serving wealthier students, he went to Pembroke College, Oxford, in 1732. Charles Wesley brought him into the Holy Club, an organization of deeply religious students which came into being in 1729. The men of this club, nicknamed Methodists by other students because of their methodical religious exercises, included also, at a later date, John Wesley. They read the Greek Testament together nightly, accepted the creeds, worked with prisoners both in the regular and debtor's prisons in the city and started a school for slum children. Their reading of the church father, Tertullian, led them into ascetic practices. These were to the detriment of Whitefield's health. Charles Wesley loaned Whitefield the book, *The Life of God in the Soul of Man*, by Henry Scougal. This book and the illness brought on by the excess of asceticism led him in 1735 into an experience of salvation by faith alone in Christ. He never forgot, however, this disciplined life and the idea of philanthropic service which he discovered in the Holy Club. As a result, his evangelism was balanced by his work on behalf of orphans in Georgia during the rest of his life.

He was ordained as a deacon of the Anglican Church by the Bishop of Gloucester in 1736. His first sermon was so evangelistic and so well received that he was accused of driving fifteen people "mad." After he received his B.A. degree that same year he went to London, where his preaching brought great crowds to his services.

A letter from John and a visit from Charles Wesley, who had just returned from Georgia, led him to a decision in 1737 to go to Georgia. He devoted the twelve months' delay to evangelistic work. During this period he collected £300 for the poor of Georgia and £1,000 for charity schools. John Wesley, who returned on the day Whitefield was to sail in 1738, cast lots and told him the lot was against his going; but Whitefield consulted his Bible and went ahead. This was the first of thirteen crossings of the Atlantic during his life.

He returned to England later in 1738 and a year later was ordained as a presbyter. During that year he attempted to raise money for a projected orphan home in Savannah. Selina, Countess of Huntingdon, became interested in him and ardently supported his work. It was at this time he began his open-air preaching to the neglected miners of Bristol who massed in crowds as large as 20,000 to hear him and to accept the Christ he proclaimed. When he had to return to London, he asked the staid Wesley to preach for him. Wesley, who thought that a soul could hardly be saved anywhere but in church, was thus induced to take up field preaching, a technique he used for the rest of his life.

Between trips to America for evangelistic work and supervision of his orphanage, Whitefield preached widely in Wales and Scotland. Through meetings in the home of the Countess of Huntingdon he was able to preach the gospel to the leaders of English society. In 1741, his followers built Moorfields Tabernacle for him in London. In all he preached about 18,000 sermons during his life. His last sermon, which was preached on September 29, 1770, from the staircase of a home where he was staying in America, lasted until the candle burned down to the socket. He died the next morning of an asthma attack.

Whitefield was the first of the trio of revivalists to be converted, to preach in the open air, to organize his converts into societies and to use lay preachers. He linked the flame of revival in the Colonies with that of the British Isles. All through his life he believed and practiced the view that the salvation of souls would have an impact upon society. He believed that a passion for souls should be linked with a humanitarian zeal. The new birth must produce fruit. This may be illustrated by an incident in which a friend lectured him for extravagance when he gave a £5 note to a poor widow. A little later a robber took his friend's money and Whitefield's coat, leaving his own rag in its place. Whitefield found £100 in the lining of the robber's coat. He reminded his friend that this was a 2000 per cent return on his gift to the widow. It seems strange that he should have had a blind spot concerning slavery, in which he apparently saw no real evil. He did, however, protest against cruel and inhuman treatment of the slaves in the Colonies.

The Countess of Huntingdon remained his staunch supporter, even through his break with Wesley in 1741 over Whitefield's acceptance of Calvinistic predestination to salvation and condemnation. She became the administrator of his societies and founded a college to train preachers at Trevecca. She employed Romaine as her chaplain and the saintly Fletcher as superintendent of her school at Trevecca. Both Lord Dartmouth and the Earl of Buchan were won to Christ through meetings in her home.

B. THE WESLEYS

John and Charles Wesley were the sons of Susannah and Samuel Wesley, both of whom came from long lines of preachers. John (1703-1791) was the fifteenth of nineteen children, eight of whom died in infancy. He earned his B.A. degree at Christchurch College, became a fellow of Lincoln College in 1726 and was ordained an Anglican minister in 1728. After two years' service as his father's assistant, he returned to his position at Lincoln College. He became an ardent member of the Holy Club, which for a time met in his rooms. In this group he saw an agency to advance the members' spiritual life and to provide means of service to their fellows.

When Oglethorpe asked for missionaries to work among the Colonists and Indians of Georgia, both Charles and John decided to go and were in that colony from 1735 to 1738. John's insistence upon the ritualism of the Anglican Church and his foolish barring of Sophia Hopkey and her husband from the communion made so much trouble for him that he had to return to England defeated and discouraged. Sophia had been formerly in love with him and he with her but, because the lot he cast ruled against marriage, Wesley gave her up. He interpreted her subsequent marriage to another and her lessened interest in religious instruction as sin.

Charles, who had come home from Georgia in 1736, saw a new life in Whitefield, and longed for the conversion experience which became his on May 21, 1738. His reading of Luther's commentary on Galatians, the visits of the Moravian Peter Böhler and the radiant life of a poor, ignorant mechanic in whose home he stayed were factors in this experience. He became the song writer of Methodism, writing over 5,500 hymns.

On May 24, the dissatisfied, longing heart of his brother John also found rest in a meeting in Nettleton Court, Aldersgate, to which he had gone unwillingly. While listening to the reading of Luther's *Preface to Paul's Epistle to the Romans,* John felt his heart "strangely warmed," trusted in Christ by faith and had an assurance that his sins had been forgiven.

Early in 1739 he started preaching in open fields at Kingswood, near Bristol, where he took over the work which Whitefield had started there. His first audience numbered about 3,000. He often preached five times a day in fields when he could find no church open to him.

He solved the problem of caring for his converts by forming church societies. This technique had been used during a seventeenth century revival and was also being used by the Moravians and by Whitefield. In this way his converts who could not count on parish clergymen for help could get it from one another and from lay preachers. He also appointed stewards to look after finances and divided the societies into classes of about twelve with a leader who collected the required one penny a week from each member and led them forward spiritually. Following the example of those in the state church who built chapels for worship, Wesley's followers built Methodist chapels where they had meetings at times when there were no regular meetings in the parish church.

Wesley never left the Anglican Church during his life, but in 1784 he took two steps which made the break inevitable after his death in 1791. He and Thomas Coke ordained two men as elders, and he consecrated Coke as the superintendent of Methodist work in North America. The Deed of Declaration in the same year created a conference of 100 ministers to hold property and to direct the work of the Methodists. This legalized the annual conference of preachers which he had begun in 1744.

Although he earned much, Wesley never spent more than £30 a year on himself and gave away as much as £1,400 in one year. His estate was less than £50 when he died. In the course of his life he traveled over 225,000 miles, most of it on horseback, and preached over 45,000 sermons, some of them two hours in length. He wrote and published 223 books and pamphlets. There were over 70,000 in the Methodist connection in England and over 43,000 in North America when he died.

Wesley, like Whitefield, believed that while salvation was an individual matter to be received by faith, it was to be social in its expression. He himself, it is estimated, gave £30,000 during his life to help other people. In 1746, he opened the first free dispensary in England for medical aid to the poor of Bristol. This remained open until 1754. He organized a Friends Society in 1785 to aid strangers in want. He wrote pamphlets against Methodists taking bribes for their vote, engaging in smuggling or swearing. He supported attempts at elementary education and the rise of Sunday schools. He opposed the slave trade bitterly and threw the support of Methodists behind every effort to destroy it. His last letter was written to Wilberforce to encourage him in the fight against that trade which he called "that execrable sum of all villanies." He visited those in prison and encouraged John Howard in his work of prison reform. Wesley neglected no opportunity to give a practical social expression to his experience of salvation by faith in Christ. And he encouraged his followers to do the same. When the great evangelical reformers needed the support of public opinion in fighting the slave trade or slavery, the Methodists would speedily forward petitions to Parliament and through gifts in the class meeting provide some of the funds necessary to obtain and disseminate information on these matters to the public.

II. THE EVANGELICAL REVIVAL

The revival which won the English lower classes under the Wesleys and Whitefield provided the troops for the army of nineteenth century social reform. The evangelical revival in the Church of England near the end of the eighteenth century contributed the leaders by winning many of the clergymen and especially wealthy, influential, middle and upper class laymen to Christ . This revival found its highest expression among clergymen such as Newton and Venn, among the members of the Clapham Sect (wealthy politicians and busi-

The Sources of Evangelical Reform

nessmen, such as Wilberforce and Thornton who lived in the suburb of Clapham Commons near London), and in the University of Cambridge through the work of Isaac Milner and Charles Simeon. Thus it will be apparent that revival in England had two separate but co-operating branches: the earlier Methodist revival among the workers of England and the later evangelical revival among the upper classes.

William Romaine was one of the first to become an Evangelical from among the Anglican clergymen who looked on the preaching of the new birth as "mere enthusiasm or fanaticism." He revised a Hebrew lexicon to which the crowned heads of Europe subscribed. His aroused vanity and ambition led him to London to seek greater glory, but instead he found Christ as His Saviour. In 1749 he was given a lectureship in St. Dunstan's Church on Fleet Street in London in which every Sunday, in spite of some opposition, he preached for forty-six years. This church became the center for London Evangelicals. In 1764 he became the rector of another church but kept up the lectureship in St. Dunstan's each Sunday evening. He was also the senior chaplain to the Countess of Huntingdon.

Henry Venn was an evangelical clergyman who ministered at Clapham, later the home of the so-called Clapham Sect, between 1754 and 1759. It was his son, John Venn, who became the parish minister of Wilberforce, Thornton and others of the Clapham Sect and for many years was their spiritual leader and advisor.

William Grimshaw of Haworth in the north of England was a young, careless, card-playing, drinking rector, who was won to Christ by the religious questions of his parishioners which he was unable to answer, the sad event of his wife's death and a book on justification by faith. Often while the congregation sang the hymn before the sermon, he would go out and round up idlers in the street or tavern and send them to church.

John Fletcher, trained for the ministry in his native Switzerland, was later converted in London. After his ordination he was sent to the poor and irreligious people of Madeley in 1760. His saintly life and earnest preaching won them to the faith.

John Newton (1725-1807), the former slave trader, was another fine representative of the evangelical clergy. As a minister in London he helped Wiberforce in his spiritual struggles prior to his conversion in 1784. And it was in Newton's home that Cowper found sympathy and understanding during some of his spells of mental distress. He was a valued advisor to the Clapham Sect in their fight against the slave trade because his experiences as a slave trader gave him authoritative information.

Newton, whose mother died when he was seven, was sent to a boarding school. When he was eleven, his father, a captain in the Mediterranean trade, took him to sea. Although Newton became very sinful, he kept alive a love for Mary Catlett whom he met when he was eighteen and she thirteen. He was forced into the navy, but through his father's influence was given a commission. He deserted his ship and finally became the servant of a West African slave trader whose Negro mistress made life miserable for Newton. Through his father's efforts he was freed. He was converted during a severe storm at sea. After his marriage to Mary Catlett, he served as captain of a slave trading ship from 1750 to 1754. This gave him firsthand knowledge of the slave trade. Giving up that odious traffic, he obtained a position in the port of Liverpool. Later, after much private study, he obtained Anglican ordination and was appointed the rector of Olney at £60 a year. John Thornton supplemented this with £200 a year and later £400 a year when Newton took Cowper into his home during the poet's mental illness. After serving at Olney from 1764 to 1779, he was called to a church in London, where he served until his death in 1807.

The Sources of Evangelical Reform 39

These influential clergymen co-operated with two evangelical leaders in the University of Cambridge, Isaac Milner and Charles Simeon. When in 1768 the authorities at Oxford expelled some evangelical students, the Evangelicals were cut off from Oxford. Thereafter, Isaac Milner, who became the head of Queen's College in 1788, made them welcome in Cambridge. Milner was a brawny north-countryman whose mental ability was so great that his examiner marked his work for the bachelor's degree as *"Incomparabilis."* Under his leadership many young Evangelicals came to Queen's College.

Milner's work was ably seconded by that of Charles Simeon. Simeon took his early training at Eton and then came to King's College at Cambridge. Here his love for horses and fancy clothes barred progress in studies. However, in preparation for required attendance at communion in 1799, he read a book on the Lord's Supper which gave such a clear presentation of the atonement that he became a Christian. After his ordination he gave his time to preaching and teaching at King's College. His classes became the focus of many evangelical ministerial students who came to Cambridge. Milner's administration and Simeon's teaching provided many Anglican evangelical pastors for the pastorates in which men like Thornton were able to place them.

Much more influential in the reforms of the era than these two teachers and the many able clergymen already described were the members of the Clapham Sect. This group consisted of wealthy evangelical laymen who lived in Clapman Commons, a village three miles from London. They were nicknamed "The Saints" by their foes in Parliament, but the name Clapham Sect came into use later as a designation for this group of men, many of whom were related by marriage.

The members of the Clapham Sect met in the home of the wealthy banker Henry Thornton who was also a member of Parliament. Their favorite meeting room was the oval library which William Pitt had designed for Thornton. Thornton, a cousin of Wilberforce, gave away each year six-sevenths of his £8,000 to £12,000 annual income. After his marriage he still gave away one-third. His father John had given away about £150,000 during his lifetime. Henry Thornton supported generously any cause which he took up. He was the first treasurer of the Church Missionary Society and the British and Foreign Bible Society. He also voluntarily paid a graduated income tax to the government.

The oldest member of the group was Granville Sharp who brought about the judicial decision which in 1772 freed slaves in England. He was also mainly responsible for the scheme to colonize Sierra Leone with the freed slaves.

Thomas Clarkson, so adept at supplying Wilberforce with information against the slave trade in the fight to end that trade (1787-1807), was another honored member of the group.

John Shore, who had been governor-general of India and who was given the title of Lord Teignmouth, was also a member. He was particularly interested in the distribution of the Bible and became the first president of the British and Foreign Bible Society in 1804.

Charles Grant had spent many years in the service of the British East India Company in India where he was noted for his financial genius. When he retired, he became a Director and later the Chairman of the Court of Directors of that company in England. His support helped Wilberforce in 1813 to get the company charter changed so that the company would have to admit missionaries to India.

James Stephen, Sr., who married Wilberforce's sister, had been a lawyer for some years in the British West Indies where he saw slavery at its worst. Upon return to a law practice in England in 1794, he became an ardent foe of the slave trade. His son, James Stephen, Jr., became an influential Colonial Undersecretary and later Colonial Secretary.

Zachary Macaulay, who lived in Clapham from 1803 to

1819, was a former plantation overseer in Jamaica and was for a time the able governor of Sierra Leone. He provided T. Fowell Buxton with much of the evidence which he used to persuade Parliament to end slavery in the British Empire in 1833, and was along with Clarkson one of the most able propagandists in the group.

Perhaps the best known of the Clapham Sect was William Wilberforce. He led the successful fight to stop the trade in slaves by the British and by many countries on the Continent. His lovable, bright personality was so attractive that his close friend, William Pitt, who never accepted Wilberforce's Christ, remained his friend even after the latter's conversion. Hannah More, who with her sisters started pioneer Sunday schools, was also a close friend of Thornton and Wilberforce, who together gave her £600 annually for her Sunday school work.

All of these men attended the services of the parish church in Clapham. John Venn, who was the rector from 1792 to 1813, provided the group with spiritual guidance. He was also the foremost promoter and founder of the Church Missionary Society, which was founded in 1799 as the missionary arm of the Evangelicals.

These wealthy and influential laymen, mostly members of the Tory party, were devout, regenerated, Bible-believing and Bible-reading Christians whose own conversions made them conscious of the spiritual need of others. They believed that the Christian was saved to serve his generation by all kinds of Christian action. This "holy village" was the most influential center of social reform and religious endeavor during the period from 1787 to 1834. The successful fight against every form of slavery was perhaps their greatest service to England. These men of piety were determined to apply the Christian ethic to national affairs in order to improve social conditions. In this manner they served as a bridge between the Dissenters, such as the Methodists, Baptists and others who supported their reform work loyally, and the Established Church in which they were lay members. They and their work were the results of the revival within the Established Church, which reached the upper class near the end of the eighteenth century as Wesley had reached the working people of England during the middle half of the century.

These men could count upon the support of what was often called the Exeter Hall influence. Exeter Hall was the meetig place in the Strand in London where most of the evangelical and Nonconformist missionary societies and other religious organizations held their annual meetings in May and June of each year. These mass meetings often sponsored protests to the government against ill-treatment of the aborigines of the Empire, or for support of movements to raise their status. These meetings on many occasions wielded enough influence to force the Colonial Office to act upon its demands. Exeter Hall influence was particularly strong during the eighteen thirties when missionary supporters co-operated with James Stephen, Jr., to bring pressure to bear for changes advantageous to natives in various colonies.

The contribution of the Evangelicals to English history only now is beginning to get the recognition it deserves from some of the foremost students of British history. Elié Halevy, a rationalistic but objective historian, was concerned with the question of why the evils of the Industrial Revolution and the dislocations of the Napoleonic wars did not evoke a revolution in England. He came to the conviction that the "operative morality" of British political liberalism expressed in reform was to be found in evangelical Christianity, especially in Methodism. This created the social sensitivity in England which was lacking in the previous century.[1] He believed that England's freedom from revolution, violent crises and sudden change was not the result of superior political institu-

---

[1] Herman Ausubel, et al., ed., *Some Modern Historians of Britain* (New York, N. Y.: Dryden Press, 1951), p. 242.

The Sources of Evangelical Reform

tions or economic organization but was the result of the eighteenth century revivals of Methodism and the Established Church which provided a new "moral cement" for a stable social order.[2] The democratic and cultural heritage of England is as much a spiritual as an economic or political achievement.

Such tributes as this by able secular as well as religious historians could be multiplied. Nowhere and at no other time can such a large body of reforms be credited to any group as the social reforms which were brought about by the leadership of the Clapham Sect and their loyal evangelical and Dissenter supporters in both the clergy and laity.

The study of these reforms, the strategy by which they were put into effect, and the spirit which was behind them can be of great value to contemporary Evangelicals. There is just as much need for reform today and for the power of Christ to be made manifest in Christians who do not divorce their Christianity from their citizenship. Revivals will still bring about the salvation of souls and service by the Christian to his culture.

---

[2]Elié Halévy, *A History of the English People, 1830-1841* (New York, N. Y.: Harcourt, Brace & Co., 1924), p. 166.

Chapter III

THE SCOPE OF EVANGELICAL REFORM

REFORM which was so badly needed in eighteenth century England was delayed for a generation by the fear of change created by the French Revolution and by the concentration of national energies upon winning the war against Napoleon. Therefore, although Wilberforce and his followers were able to bring about a ban on the slave trade by Englishmen in 1807, it was not until after 1815 that the dynamic of religion began to produce a widespread impact.

I. SPIRITUAL AND PHYSICAL FREEDOM FOR COLORED PEOPLES

A. SPIRITUAL MEASURES FOR FREEING COLORED MEN

Measures for the spiritual blessing of the colored subjects of England were as much a matter of concern to the social reformers, such as the members of the Clapham Sect, as were measures for their physical freedom. This concern for the spiritual development of subject colored peoples was intensified as England gained colonies during the eighteenth century. In 1763, England emerged as the victor over all her imperial rivals in the struggle for colonies. Apart from the Moravians of Saxony, who had a deep interest in missions after 1732, the English were the first to organize missionary societies to take the gospel to the colored people. The Dissenters, particularly the Baptists, were the leaders in this movement.

William Carey (1761-1834) is given the credit for launching modern English missionary activities. Carey was a Baptist cobbler at Moulton in the English Midlands. He also served as pastor of a Baptist chapel. The study of several foreign languages (for which he had real aptitude), the reading of travel books and the writings of Eliot and Brainerd created in him a sense of obligation to the pagan world. He expressed this in his pamphlet, "An Inquiry into the Obligation of Christians to Use Means for the Conversion of the Heathen," which was published in 1792. In a sermon on Isaiah 54:2, 3 to the Northampton Baptist Association meeting on May 21, 1792, he urged the obligation of foreign missions upon his colleagues. He asserted that one should "Expect great things from God; attempt great things for God." This endeavor led to the founding at Kettering on October 2, 1792, of the Baptist Missionary Society with an initial budget of £12, 2s. 6d. Carey became its first candidate and went out to India in 1793. He was put in charge of an indigo factory but used his spare time to do missionary work and to translate the Scripures into the native dialect.

The founding of the predominantly Congregationalist London Missionary Society in 1795 was inspired to some extent by a letter from William Carey in July, 1794, to Dr. Ryland, a minister of Bristol. He shared this letter with three other ministers.

Further impetus for organization of the society came from a review of Melville Horne's book, *Letters on Missions Addressed to Protestant Ministers of the British Churches.* At the end of the review, printed in the September, 1794, issue of *Evangelical Magazine,* the reviewer Haweis stated that he had £600 (his own gift of £500 and the promise of another £100) to equip six missionaries for work in the South Sea Islands. This moved John Eyre, the editor, to discuss the matter with Matthew Wilks. The two began a bi-monthly meeting at the Castle and Falcon Inn in Aldersgate Street to discuss and to pray for missions.

At a meeting of several ministers in November, 1794, the decision was reached to issue a call for the organization of a missionary society. Thirty-four ministers met on February 17, 1795, and signed a statement that they would work for the establishment of a missionary society. At a meeting on September 21 at the Castle and Falcon, John Eyre read his paper on a plan for a society. The organization meeting took place the next day in the Spa Fields Chapel with over 200 ministers present. Directors were selected on September 23, the Castle and Falcon made the meeting-place of the directors, and the South Sea Islands and later Africa were decided upon as the spheres of service.

It was this society under which John Philip, Robert Moffat, David Livingstone and John Mackenzie were to do their great work. Missionaries, who were to civilize as well as convert the natives, were left free to chose the form of church government they thought was most suitable. Wilberforce, though an Anglican, became a life member of this London Missionary Society in 1796 by a gift of £10.10s.

Another interdenominational society, the Glasgow Missionary Society, was founded by the Scottish churches in 1796.

Because the Society for the Propagation of the Gospel (Anglican) was working only in the British American colonies and in the West Indies, members of the Clapham Sect decided that there should be a society through which Evangelicals in the Church of England could support missionary work in Africa and elsewhere. Their Church Missionary Society grew out of the meetings of the Eclectic Society which was made up of evangelical clergy and laity meeting together after 1786 to discuss missions. John Venn, the rector of the Clapham Commons church, insisted that the new society should be in the Established Church and should be Evangelical in doctrine. Largely under his inspiration, a group of sixteen clergymen and nine laymen met on April 12, 1799, in the Castle and Falcon Inn, Aldersgate Street, an inn owned by Dupont, a member of the Spa Fields Chapel. They organized the Society for Missions to Africa and the East. In 1812 it was renamed the Church Missionary Society. Most of the men of the Clapham Sect were at this organizational meeting. Henry Thornton was made the treasurer, and John Venn was made the chairman of the meeting. Henry Martyn, the society's first English volunteer, went out to India in 1805 as a chaplain to the East India Company employees but engaged in missionary work among the nationals in his spare time. It was this society which later opened missions in New Zealand and which did missionary work in Uganda and brought about the acceptance of Uganda as a protectorate by the British government. The Church Missionary Society was the missionary arm of the Clapham Sect in the early part of the nineteenth century.

The Methodists were not to be outdone and in 1813 informally organized the Wesleyan Missionary Society which developed into a formally organized society in 1817. They sent missionaries to the west coast of Africa where most of them died with fever. Zachary Macaulay, governor of Sierra Leone, had difficulty with some of the early Methodist missionaries sent to that colony because they were not well chosen. Undaunted, the society continued its work and earned an honorable place in the history of British missions.

These societies had excellent organizations. England was divided into districts and in each district there were branch societies in individual churches. Each group had its own weekly and monthly meetings, treasurer and subscriptions. This formidable organization, whether of the evangelical Anglicans or the dissenting churches, could be counted upon to support by petition, by pleas to their representatives in Parliament, or by money the humanitarian activities of the

Clapham Sect and its allies in Parliament in order to obtain action favorable to the interests of natives in British colonies. The directors of these societies through reports from missionaries in the field often had more reliable information than the Colonial Office had and could use it through their magazines or annual meetings each spring in Exeter Hall to bring the maximum pressure to bear upon the government to win support for their cause. The missionaries of these societies upheld and exemplified higher ethical standards than the white traders and worked for the well-being of their native charges. Missionary societies to convert the heathen worked hand in hand with the social reformers in the crusade to end slavery and to protect the aborigines of Africa and of the Pacific islands.

The members of the Clapham Sect also believed that the Bible must be put into the hands both of the English people and the natives in the colonies if its power to change lives was to be released. Thomas Charles, a Welsh Methodist, told members of the Religious Tract Society on December 7, 1802, of the need for Bibles in that part of Britain. He urged the organization of a society to distribute Bibles. Joseph Hughes, a Baptist minister who had heard of a Welsh girl who walked thirty miles to obtain a Bible, urged that the proposed Bible Society should be as broad as the need for Bibles in the world. A committee from the Religious Tract Society approached Charles Grant, and on February 2, 1803, a breakfast meeting was held at Wilberforce's home with Grant, Henry Thornton, who was already spending £2,000 a year on the distribution of Bibles, and others present. By January 10, 1804, the name English and Foreign Bible Society was decided upon and the committee called a public meeting to launch the Society. At a meeting on March 7, 1804, with Granville Sharp in the chair, the Society was formally organized.

At a later meeting in May, 1804, John Shore (Lord Teignmouth) was elected president and Henry Thornton treasurer. Shore, who had served the British East India Company for years as an expert on fiscal matters, was for a time a member of that company's Board of Control in England. He made the Society his major interest until his presidency was terminated by death in 1834. The Society had an annual income of £50,000 by 1812. When slaves throughout the British Empire were freed in 1834, it gave 100,000 copies of the New Testament and Psalms to the freedmen. The men of the Clapham Sect realized that only as the Word was made available would faith be placed in the Christ whom it proclaimed.

As early as 1793, Wilberforce and the "Saints" of the Clapham Sect became concerned with the fact that the British East India Company was deliberately keeping India closed to missionaries, although it did permit entrance of chaplains to Europeans in India. Adoniram Judson, who had intended to labor in India, was forced to leave there and went to Burma instead. Carey had also faced difficulty in getting to India. When the charter of the company came up for renewal in Parliament in 1793, Wilberforce and his friends battled to have a clause included which would have committed the company to the admission and encouragement of missionaries, but they were unsuccessful.

When the charter was presented for renewal in 1813, they had been perparing for over a year to have it changed to open India to missions. Wilberforce interviewed Perceval, the Prime Minister, who was an Evangelical; Gisbourne was given the task of stirring up the clergy; Zachary Macaulay prepared circulars for the general public; Babington was given the task of organizing petitions to Parliament; and the aid of the Church Missionary Society was enlisted in a special meeting of 400 gentlemen. Public meetings, petitions, letters to *The Times* of London, interviews with influential people by Wilberforce, and pressure through Grant upon the Court of Directors of the Company were used. By these means they helped put into effect the resolution proposed in Parliament in 1793 that means ought to be adopted to lead gradually to the advance of the Indians in useful knowledge, religion and morals.

On June 22, 1813, Wilberforce spoke for three hours on a resolution stating that it was England's duty to promote "the interest and happiness" of the Indians by measures to introduce them to "useful knowledge and moral improvement." This would be done through people who should be admitted as missionaries to India under the protection of British law. He was backed by 837 petitions bearing over 500,000 names. The pressure of Christian public opinion was enough to persuade Parliament that the new charter should have provisions for the free entry of missionaries to India under license from the Board of Control which could overrule the Court of Directors of the Company, for an archbishop and three archdeacons for India as well as three chaplains of the Church of Scotland. India was thus opened to missions, and Christianity by law was given a place as one of the religions of India in spite of the opposition of the company. Parliament for the first time also granted about £10,000 annually for education in India. Wilberforce wrote of this project as "the greatest" to employ "the heart of man."

Perhaps Wilberforce would not have been so successful if he had not had the support of Charles Grant (1746-1823), another member of the Clapham Sect. Grant went to India in 1767 and rapidly accumulated gambling debts of £20,000 before his conversion in 1776, which was brought about by a tragedy in the family. A letter from the Methodist minister, Coke, in 1784 enlisted his interest in missions. In 1792, he wrote a pamphlet pleading for missions in India. Before his return to England in 1790, all the trade of the British East India Company in Bengal was in his hands, and the governor-general, Cornwallis, expressed the utmost confidence in him. He became a member of the Court of Directors in 1797 and

The Scope of Evangelical Reform 51

in 1805 its chairman. He helped Henry Martyn and other evangelical chaplains to get to India where they could do some missionary work on the side.

Some conceive of the missionary's task as only the conversion of the souls of the natives, but the early nineteenth century British missionaries engaged in several other activities, such as education, politics and experimental agriculture as legitimate means to the desired end, the conversion of the souls. One such means to open the new lands to the gospel was missionary exploration. Such men as Campbell in South Africa, Rebmann and Kraph in East Africa, Livingstone in Central Africa and Grenfell in the Congo were great missionary explorers. Up to the time of Livingstone, the map of interior Africa was filled with pictures of curious creatures or was a blank as far as European knowledge of the interior was concerned. Missionaries were the earliest explorers, especially David Livingstone in Central Africa. The topographical nature of the interior was discovered and trade routes were opened up. Secular explorers, who had their curiosity aroused by the missionary-explorers, completed the work begun by missionaries.

John Campbell, minister of a church in London, was sent out from 1812 to 1814 and again from 1818 to 1821 as a visiting inspector to survey the work of conversion and civilization of the natives done by the London Missionary Society in South Africa. In addition to his work of inspection, on his first trip he spent six weeks exploring the Orange River. He is credited with putting on the map rather accurately the course of the Orange River and with discovering the sources of the Limpopo River in 1820. By these discoveries he hoped to extend further to the north the scope of missionary activity of the Society among the natives.

Reports of snow-capped mountains and large inland lakes sent back to the Church Missionary Society office in London by their German missionaries, Krapf, Rebmann and Erhardt, stimulated exploration of East Africa in order to find the sources of the Nile. In the spring of 1848, on a trip to the interior, Rebmann discovered the snow-capped mountain of Kilimanjaro, just a short distance south of the equator. His report to the C. M. S. was published in the May 1849 issue of the *Church Missionary Intelligencer*. Krapf was the first white man to see Mount Kenya on a trip which he made in 1849. Erhardt, who also made trips into the interior, heard of a great lake in the interior. He put this data on a map showing the supposed location of the lake. This map of the inland sea was published in the missionary society's magazine and later in the *Proceedings* of the Royal Geographical Society for 1856. The lake on his map covered the area of the actual great lakes of central Africa. These explorations and this map stimulated others to find the great lake which had been pictured. In all these endeavors exploration for curiosity's sake was subordinated to a desire to find new ways to the interior to open up missionary stations. But in the Providence of God their work led to the discovery of the sources of the Nile and the great lakes system of Central Africa.

The greatest of all the missionary explorers was David Livingstone (1813-1873), whose interest was in blazing trails along which the Gospel could travel northward into the heart of Africa. He studied medicine with the idea of becoming a doctor in England until, in 1831, he read the appeal of Charles Gutzlaff for medical missionaries in China. In 1837, after narrowly escaping rejection by the Society because of his ineptitude at public prayer and preaching, he was accepted as a medical missionary of the London Missionary Society.

While waiting for the Opium War against China to end, he heard Robert Moffat of Africa preach. Moffat told him of the challenge of thousands of unreached native kraals, and Livingstone decided to go as a medical missionary to Africa.

The Scope of Evangelical Reform

After completing his medical examinations and being ordained, he left for Africa in 1840. On the voyage he demonstrated his interest in his environment by learning the art of taking nautical observations from the captain. He married Mary Moffat and they settled down on a missionary station.

With some English sportsmen, he traveled north in the summer of 1849 and discovered Lake Ngami. His topographical and botanical reports were given by a friend to the Royal Geographical Society which voted Livingstone £25 and thanks. Livingstone wryly wondered whether by mistake they had not left off a zero. In 1851 another expedition with his friends led to the discovery of the upper part of the Zambezi River. It was here he saw the horrors of the Arab slave trade for the first time. Because his children needed education and might not survive in the fever-laden areas he wanted to explore, he sent his family home and carried on his difficult explorations alone. He hoped to find roads leading from the center of Africa to both east and west coasts.

In 1853 he traveled north again and, by May, 1854, was the first white man to reach the west coast of Africa by travel from the interior. He was offered a free trip home on a British warship but would not go because he had promised to take his Makololo carriers back to their homes in the interior. This he did. Swamps, fever and forests made the road to the west impracticable. He traveled to the east coast in 1855 and 1856. It was on this trip that he discovered and named the majestic Victoria Falls of the Zambezi River. These two trips gave him the distinction of being the first white man to cross equatorial Africa.

Upon his return to England he was honored by many groups and his book, *Missionary Travels and Researches,* aroused great interest in Africa. He was then sent out by the government at the head of an expedition to survey and explore the country watered by the lower Zambezi. On this trip he discovered Lake Nyasa. This expedition lasted from 1858 to 1863, when it was recalled by the government. By this time his desire to open up Central Africa to missions had become subordinate to his desire to expose and to destroy, by legitimate trade between the natives and Britain, the Portuguese and Arab slave trade which he had seen in all his journeys.

The costs of his final trip were borne jointly by the government, the Royal Geographical Society and his friends. This trip between 1866 and his death in 1873 resulted in the discovery of Lakes Mweru and Bangweola, but he did not succeed in his ambition to discover the sources of the Nile.

His death on his knees on May 1, 1873, stopped his active work, but his influence lived on. Central Africa had been opened to legitimate commerce and missions, and he had so publicized the slave trade that the awakened conscience of English Christianity did not rest until that trade was suppressed. His challenge to the churches at home led to the founding of the Universities Mission to Central Africa and the Livingstonia Mission of the Scottish Presbyterians as well as the Blantyre Mission of the Established Church of Scotland. He can rightly be considered as the greatest of all explorers of Africa.

The exploration work of the Baptist Missionary Society centers upon the activities of George Grenfell (1849-1906). From 1880 until his death in 1906 he was busy exploring and mapping the Congo and its tributaries. In 1884 he discovered the mouth of the Mubangi River, the greatest tributary of the Congo. His careful observations led to the publication by the Royal Geographical Society in 1887 of his chart of the Congo between Leopoldville and the Stanley Falls. For this he was awarded the Founder's Gold Medal of the Society. In exploration of the Congo his name is second only to that of Stanley who had been so impressed by Livingstone when he had met him during Livingstone's final trip.

The Scope of Evangelical Reform

These geographical feats were always means to the great end, the evangelization of Africa, and were often incidental to other heavy missionary activities. They were accomplished with small means and at great sacrifice, but these men thought them worthwhile in the spread of the Gospel.

Missionaries on occasion became road builders. They sought to make the way into the interior easier for others and to foster legitimate commerce so that the native chiefs would not have to sell their people for goods which they wanted.

Alexander Mackay, of the Church Missionary Society in Uganda, built a rough road from the coast to the interior, a distance of nearly 250 miles. It was nothing more than a widened trail for bullocks, with rough bridges and lessened grades in steep places, but it served its purpose until it was replaced by a shorter, better road.

A still more extensive job of road building was done by the engineer James Stewart, a cousin of the James Stewart who founded Lovedale in South Africa for industrial education of the natives. He spent his furlough from engineering work in India with the Scottish Presbyterians in Nyasaland in 1877. He became so interested in their work that he gave up his position with an annual salary of £500 to become a missionary-engineer. After a preliminary survey by Stewart in 1879, James Stevenson, a Glasgow merchant, gave £4,000 to build a road to connect the north end of Lake Nyasa with the south end of Lake Tanganyika. Stewart died in 1883 after constructing 26 miles of the most difficult section of the road. It was completed by others and served the missionaries and Christian traders of the African Lakes Company well for many years. These were the first roads of any account in the interior of Africa. Their builders felt they were serving Christ well in providing such means to speed and to ease missionary travel.

B. Freeing Colored Men from Physical Slavery

Missionary and Bible societies, legislation by Evangelicals in England to open lands such as India to missions, and exploration and road-building by missionaries were all used as means to convert and civilize the native in his own land. What was to be done about the Negroes who had become slaves in the British dominions, and about the trade which had made them slaves? The Evangelicals also met the tremendous social challenge of slavery with all the spiritual vigor and political power at their disposal. One who has read the sources on the matter is impressed with the Christian zeal and sincerity of these men in their fight to end the evil traffic.

English participation in the slave trade began in 1562 with the activities of John Hawkins. He secured over 300 slaves from captured Spanish slave ships and sold them to the Spanish in the West Indies for over $125 per person. Between 1564 and 1565 Queen Elizabeth gave him four ships with 170 men. This expedition took 400 slaves to the Spanish Colonies and made profits of 60 per cent. In 1663 the Company of Royal Adventurers of England Trading with Africa was chartered to obtain slaves to sell to the colonies in the West Indies. Between 1680 and 1700, 300,000 slaves were carried in British ships. The Asiento agreement in the Treaty of Utrecht, which ended the War of the Spanish Succession in 1713, gave England the right to supply 4,800 slaves annually for thirty years to the Spanish colonies. The Spanish and English rulers were each to get a quarter of the profits. In 1750 the slave trade was thrown open to any British trader who wanted to engage in it.

By 1770 it is estimated that over half of the total slaves were carried in 192 British ships with space for about 50,000 slaves. By this date Liverpool men had more than half of the trade and six-sevenths by 1800. Between 1789 and 1793

The Scope of Evangelical Reform

Liverpool ships carried over 300,000 slaves to the West Indies and obtained over £15 million for them. Over two million slaves were brought to the Thirteen Colonies and the West Indies between 1680 and 1786.

The holds of the ships were divided horizontally by decks about three feet apart with a corridor down the center. The slaves were forced into these "shelves" in handcuffs or chained in pairs and taken out only for forced exercise. One can imagine the stench and filth and disease in these ships in the humid waters off Africa. An average of one slave in six died on the voyage, and in 1800 it was estimated that for every "seasoned" field hand in the colonies one died or was killed. British slave ships and British slavery had a much worse reputation than the more humane Spanish slave system which was modified by the efforts of the church of that land.

The vested interests involved may be seen in the fact that the ships carried Lancashire cotton goods to Africa to trade for slaves. These slaves were then carried to the British colonies in America and the West Indies where they were exchanged for raw cotton, tobacco and sugar which was then taken to England. In 1791, a Colonel Tarleton claimed in the House of Commons that banning the trade to Englishmen would kill a trade of about 160 ships, 5,500 sailors, £800,000 worth of slaves and West Indian commerce valued at £6 million. The West Indian lobby saw its profits from the slave trade endangered by abolition and moved to protect their vested interests. A slave ship might clear £60,000 on one voyage with profits averaging 15 per cent on the investment. It is estimated that the Liverpool Corporation spent over £10,000 in the bitter fight against the abolitionists. This economic interest was reinforced by the idea that the sailors trained on slave ships would strengthen the navy in time of war. These strong vested interests fought bitterly against Wilberforce, Buxton and their supporters in the attempts to abolish first the slave trade and then slavery in all British possessions. The Christian crusade against slavery was won only after a fifty-year struggle.

The Quakers and the Methodists were among the earliest in the eighteenth century to protest against slavery and the slave trade. These early protests were of a spiritual rather than a political or humanitarian nature. As early as 1671 George Fox told the Quakers of Barbados to be kind to their slaves and after some years to free them. In 1761 any English Quaker engaged in the slave trade was disowned by the Society if he persisted in such trade. Thus did the Quakers act as a body against the trade, the only religious community to do so up to this time.

Anthony Benezet, a Quaker, wrote three books against slavery between 1762 and 1767. It was likely his pamphlet, *Historical Account of Guinea* (1767), which so affected Thomas Clarkson in his determination to abolish the slave trade. It was also one of his books which aroused Wesley's determination to fight slavery. Wesley wrote on February 12, 1772, that he had read a book by "an honest Quaker" regarding "that execrable sum of all villanies," the slave trade. He thought that there was nothing so bad in history, not even the sufferings of Christians who were Mohammedan slaves. Benezet, who was of Huguenot stock, became a Quaker after he and his parents migrated to America. He gave up his business and taught in Penn's school in Philadelphia.

In 1774, two years after the historic court decision which freed slaves in England, John Wesley actively entered the anti-slavery fight with the publication of his book, *Thoughts Upon Slavery*, which ran through three editions during its first year. He had seen something of slavery during his sojourn in Georgia from 1735 to 1738. In his book Wesley contrasted the idyllic life of the Negro in Africa with the injustice of enslaving fellow-creatures. To him slavery was not necessary for economic gain. Both owner and slave must one day give an account to God for this life. This book brought

The Scope of Evangelical Reform 59

the support of Wesley and his Methodist followers to the side of the anti-slavery leaders in their long fight against slavery. By letter, sermon, petition or boycott of slave-grown sugar, the Methodists solidly supported all efforts at abolition.

In 1787, Wesley wrote a long letter against slavery to the *Arminian Magazine*. On August 18, 1787, in a letter to Samuel Hoare, a London banker, he mentioned that he received a letter from Clarkson in which Clarkson stated his intention to try to obtain an act of Parliament abolishing slavery on the plantations in the colonies. Wesley wrote that the Methodists in America had already set hundreds of slaves free, "a little stand against this shocking abomination." He thought that if Clarkson's plan could be carried out it would be "a lasting honor" to Great Britain. He told Hoare that he and his friends would face terrific opposition but should remember that with God all things are possible. He added that he would help all he could and would reprint his *Thoughts Upon Slavery* to which he would add a note favoring Clarkson's idea of abolition. He also wrote a long letter to Granville Sharp on October 11, 1787, stating that he had detested the slave trade since he first heard of it, but now hated it more so after reading Sharp's writings upon it. He told him that he would do everything in his power to help the work of their Anti-slavery Society. In a letter of November 24, 1787, to Thomas Funnell he informed him that he had published "a large edition" of his book, which he had promised Hoare he would do, and had sent copies to every part of England.

Wesley's courage in this fight is shown by his announcement in Bristol on a Tuesday evening in 1788 that he would preach on slavery on Thursday evening. He had a packed house in this port city from which slave ships set forth, and he announced that Friday would be set apart as a day of fasting and prayer that God would free the slaves.

On February 4, 1789, Wesley reported in his *Journals* that Wilberforce had called upon him and wrote that they had a fine conversation. Wilberforce, in mentioning the meeting, said that he had called on Wesley whom he described as "a fine old fellow." Wilberforce and two friends many years later gave an annuity of £60 to Charles Wesley's widow for thirty years until her death. Wesley's last letter, dated February 24, 1791, was to Wilberforce, urging him to fight against the slave trade. Wesley added that unless Wilberforce had divine support he would be worn out in this struggle by the opposition "of men and devils."

These promises of support were not meaningless. The abolitionists would have had a hard time without the aid of the Methodists and other Dissenters. In 1792, when Wilberforce called for petitions supporting his resolution in the House of Commons for abolition of the slave trade, the Methodists alone produced 229,426 signatures while 21 other dissenting groups and Roman Catholics produced 100,000 fewer names. In 1833, when efforts were being made to abolish slavery, 224,000 of 354,000 Dissenters signing petitions were Methodists. When in 1806 it seemed that Wilberforce might lose his seat, influential Methodists and circuit ministers of York each sent out circulars urging his election. This intervention was one of the main reasons Wilberforce was able to hold his seat.

The late eighteenth century revival in the Established Church may have produced the leaders in the anti-slavery army, the men of the Clapham Sect, but it was the earlier Methodist revival which provided the troops in that army. Men who had become sons of God by faith in Christ could not bear to see potential or actual sons of God remain in physical slavery. Their personal faith expressed itself in Christian action in society.

The Scope of Evangelical Reform

1. *Abolition of Slavery in England and Colonization of Ex-slaves in Sierra Leone, 1772-1807*

The struggle of these earnest Christians against English slavery began with the work of Granville Sharp (1735-1813) who in 1772 was successful in his attempt to have slavery outlawed in England. Sharp came from a line of theologians that went back to Puritanism in the seventeenth century. His grandfather had been Archbishop of Canterbury in the reign of Anne. His father was an authority on Greek and Hebrew.

Because the family was so large, Sharp was not financially able to attend University but was apprenticed to various linen drapers after his high school work. While an apprentice he argued religion with a fellow-apprentice who referred to the Greek New Testament. Sharp learned Greek in order to answer him and later wrote a still valid tract on the significance of the Greek article in the New Testament. To refute a Jewish fellow-apprentice who quoted Hebrew, Sharp learned Hebrew and wrote a pamphlet on the use of an important Hebrew word. When his friend Henry Willoughby discovered he had a claim to the barony of Willoughby de Parham, Sharp looked up and verified the claim so that Willoughby got his barony and went to the House of Lords. Sharp finished his apprenticeship in 1757 but failed as a draper.

A friend, Captain Stockdale, got him a civil service position in 1758 in the Ordnance Office at the Tower of London at £40 a year. After work Sharp would study prophecy in Daniel and Revelation or go to his wealthy brother's home where the whole family would meet to play and sing. In fact, they had a family orchestra which performed before the king. They loved Handel's music particularly and used to end their concerts with his "Hallelujah Chorus." From the above it is clear that Sharp would put every energy into a project until he could complete it.

Sharp began to study the subject of slavery in England when in 1765 he met the slave Jonathan Strong who had come for free treatment to Sharp's doctor-brother William. The two nursed Strong back to health after the brutal beating his master David Lisle, a lawyer of Barbados, had given him. They got Strong a job with a druggist.

Two years later Lisle saw his now healthy slave and sold him to James Kerr, a Jamaica planter, for £30. Strong was put in prison for safe keeping by his new owner. When Sharp got word, he told the jailer not to give up the slave and brought the case before the Lord Mayor of London. Kerr's attorney claimed the slave on the strength of the bill of sale, but the Lord Mayor released Strong. When Captain Laird (transporting for Kerr) tried to seize Strong to take him to his ship, Sharp threatened a suit for assault. Kerr and Laird sued Sharp for damages for unlawfully holding another's property. Sharp's lawyers advised him to pay because an opinion in 1729 by Yorke and Talbot, Law Officers of the Crown, stated that a baptized slave living in England did not become free nor did his master lose his right to hold him as property nor his right to compel him to return to the colonies.

Sharp studied constitutional law for the next two years and found in an early edition of Blackstone's *Commentaries* an opinion based on an older case that a Negro became free when he entered England. This opinion was omitted in later editions. He drew up a long memorandum on the case and sent twenty copies of it to the centers of legal education, the Inns of Court. This memo so frightened Kerr's and Lisle's lawyers that they delayed the case until they had to pay triple costs for not bringing suit. Sharp published this memo in 1769 as a tract, "The Injustices of Tolerating Slavery in England."

This layman had proved to be cleverer than the lawyers of England. Lord Mansfield, the Lord Chief Justice, in a later case which Sharp instituted, dismissed it on the ground that

The Scope of Evangelical Reform

the owner brought no proof that the slave Thomas Lewis was his property. He did this rather than pass upon Sharp's argument that slaves became free when they landed in England. He also wanted to protect the £700,000 investment in over 14,000 Negro slaves in England.

Sharp's chance came in 1772 when James Somersett, a Negro, was rescued from a ship on which he was put for sale as a slave in Jamaica. Because Somersett was clearly his master's property, Lord Mansfield was forced to give an opinion on the point of Sharp's contention. On June 22, 1772, Mansfield gave his decision that slavery was so odious that nothing but positive law could support it. Because there was no such positive law, Sharp's contention that slavery could not be permitted in England was correct. He therefore freed Somersett and by the same legal principle freed over 14,000 other slaves in England.

It must be remembered that Sharp carried on all this work along with his regular job in the Ordnance Office and, in fact, was promoted in 1774 to become an assistant to the Secretary of the Ordnance. When arms were sent to the British army in America, Sharp thought they might be used to kill American Quakers and protested. He was allowed two leaves of absence for six months because he was such a valuable man, but finally resigned in 1775. His wealthy brothers, James and William, gave him support for the rest of his life so he could devote himself to humanitarian projects.

Sharp's study of the Old Testament convinced him that slavery was wrong. Then he began to study the institution in the colonies. By 1779 his canvass of the hierarchy of the Church of England revealed that he had the support of nearly all of them against the slave trade. He joined with Thomas Clarkson, who had given up the ministry to devote his life to the defeat of the slave trade. Sharp emphasized the ethical aspects of slavery as a sin against God which would bring divine retribution upon England.

The case of the *Zong* pointed up the horrible truth that Negroes were articles of commerce. Luke Collingwood in 1781 sailed the *Zong* from West Africa to Jamaica with over 400 slaves on board. Several were ill and might have infected the others. Using the jettison clause in the insurance contract which read that, if part of cargo had to be thrown out to save the rest, the insurance company would pay for that part lost, he drove 132 sick slaves overboard. The trial was not for murder, which Sharp wanted, but whether throwing the slaves overboard was a genuine jettison or fraud upon the insurance company. The case was dismissed.

In 1787 he, James Ramsay, a clergyman from Saint Christopher who hated slavery, four Quakers and others formed the first Abolition Committee—to stop the slave trade. Though Sharp was its chairman, he took little part in the committee as he felt that slavery rather than just the slave trade should be abolished. He did, however, help to initiate and supported the founding of Sierra Leone as a colony to which freed slaves might be sent to start life anew instead of being beggars in England.

The first British colony in Africa was the result of the energy and idealism of the "Saints." Something had to be done to keep 14,000 slaves who had been freed by the judicial decision of 1772 from becoming vagabonds or a public charge. These Christians felt that the abolition of slavery should be tied in with Christianity, commerce and colonization. A Dr. Henry Smeathman, who had been a naturalist in Sierra Leone for some years, proposed in 1786 that the free slaves should be settled there. Sharp took up the idea as the logical solution of the problem. The government, to get rid of the ex-slaves, gave £12 per head to transport the ex-slaves to their new home, and in February, 1787, the expedition sailed with 411 settlers. In May the leaders made a treaty with the nearest chief for twenty square miles of land which was divided into lots for the settlers. By March of 1788, only 130 settlers

The Scope of Evangelical Reform 65

were alive, and they were only saved by provisions which Sharp sent out at his own expense. Trouble with a native chief led to the burning of the settler's town in 1789.

The project was expanded when in 1790 Wilberforce, Thornton and other "Saints" organized the Saint George's Bay Association with Sharp as president and Thornton as chairman. In 1791 Thornton, who had made the project his main responsibility, reorganized the Association as the Sierra Leone Company and secured a charter from the government. The town was rebuilt, and naval units under Lieutenant Clarkson, a brother of the great researcher, Thomas Clarkson, took over 1,100 Negroes, who had fought for the British during the American Revolution and who had settled in Nova Scotia, to Sierra Leone. Lieutenant Clarkson became the first governor of the new colony. By 1794 there were 200 houses and 1,400 settlers. The colony suffered a temporary setback in 1794 when French sailors destroyed every home, sacked the town and seized goods worth £10,000 which had just arrived for the colony. Zachary Macaulay served as governor from 1794 to 1799 and put the colony on a firm foundation. By 1807 the financial resources of the company were about exhausted. Henry Thornton himself lost over £2,000 in the venture, and the £240,000 of subscribed captial was lost, but by 1825, Sierra Leone was the new home of 18,000 slaves. The government dissolved the Company and on the first day of 1808 the arca became Sierra Leone, the first British colony in Africa.

Even though Sharp was emotional, erratic and, therefore, no leader, his capacity for tireless research on problems in which he was interested, his love of the Bible and his attractive personality made him a useful servant of Christ. His one great love was the study of the prophetic Scriptures. This study led him in 1805 to write a tract identifying the Roman Catholic church with the Babylon described in the Book of Revelation, but he did look for a future perfect millennial order. The judicial decision of 1772 freeing slaves in England and the development of Sierra Leone were his great contributions.

2. The Abolition and Suppression of the European Slave Trade, 1787-1807

The names of Wilberforce and Clarkson shine with particular luster in this part of the story of the social activities of the Clapham Sect. Thomas Clarkson (1760-1846) gave his life over completely to the crusade to abolish slavery. Not a leader of men, he chose to work behind the scenes gathering accurate information for Wilberforce and his friends. Much of Wilberforce's success in the House of Commons came from his use of facts which Clarkson supplied him.

Clarkson was the son of a headmaster of a private high school. He graduated from Cambridge in 1783 with a first in mathematics. Two years later he entered an essay contest on the topic, "On the Slavery and Commerce of the Human Species, Particularly the African." His Latin essay was entitled "Is it lawful to make slaves of others against their will?" When he read his essay in the Senate House at Cambridge, he received much applause and won the prize. The next year he translated it into English and had it published by a friendly Quaker publisher. This brought him to the favorable attention of James Ramsay and Sharp.

Thinking of this essay as he rode home in the summer of 1785, Clarkson got off his horse. On his knees he dedicated himself to the cause of the slave. This led him to give up a promising clerical career to become the researcher for abolition. His temperate, persistent, accurate search for facts was needed if this little band of Christians was to win the public to its cause.

In his search for accurate information on slavery, Clarkson got help from James Ramsay. Ramsay, pastor of a church in Kent, had spent nineteen years on Saint Christopher in the

The Scope of Evangelical Reform

West Indies where he had opportunity to obtain firsthand information on slavery.

Clarkson also visited the slave ship, the *Fly,* in London and was filled with "melancholy and horror" at what he saw. He found that on one voyage there had been a 50 per cent mortality rate among the slaves and that 20 per cent of the sailors engaged in the trade died in one year.

In all, it is estimated that Clarkson traveled 35,000 miles to get evidence. On one occasion, as he stepped off a ship onto the dock, he saw several sailors from a Liverpool slave ship walking toward him with locked arms in order to push him off the dock. He picked out the weakest-looking man in the line and was able to break it and get away safely. Had they been successful he would have been "accidentally" drowned or labeled a "suicide." Thus his work was not without danger to himself. In 1789 Wilberforce at his own expense sent Clarkson to Paris for six months upon the outbreak of the French Revolution in order to persuade the National Assembly to abolish the French slave trade. Clarkson wrote long twenty-page letters to Mirabeau every day of a hot summer month to inform him on slavery.

When he first met Wilberforce, the latter told Clarkson that the topic of the abolition of slavery was near his heart. Later when he went to ask Wilberforce to lead the pro-abolition forces, Clarkson was so overwhelmed by the significance of his mission that he came away without saying anything. In May, 1787, the Society for the Abolition of the Slave Trade was formed to obtain and to publish evidence showing the need for abolition. From this time on Clarkson became the chief researcher and propagandist for the forces of abolition.

His second work after the publication of his prize-winning pamphlet in 1786 was a pamphlet on the slave trade and the possible consequences of abolition. He went alone to Bristol and Liverpool and got samples of products made by Africans, information on the methods of slave capture, witnesses who would testify in Parliament, information on the losses of sailors in the trade and specimens of thumb-screws and the speculum used to open forcibly the mouths of slaves in order to feed them when they attempted to court death by starvation. This trip took five months and the subsequent use of his facts was the first employment of public propaganda on such a large scale. In 1789 he produced the first published plan of a slave ship.

He spent £1,600 of his own money in his investigation without hopes of regaining it, but he was later reimbursed by subscriptions of £100 from Wilberforce, £50 from Wedgwood, the head of the famed Wedgwood china firm, and others. His work may be summed up as the securing of witnesses for the investigations of slave trading by committees of the government, keeping Wilberforce supplied with accurate data for his speeches in the House, and expert propagandizing of the country to create public opinion which would force parliamentary action. It is little wonder his health broke in 1794 and he had to retire from the struggle for a time. He had, however, fulfilled his mission of discovering and giving to the English public a true picture of the trade. Upon request he wrote the two-volume book, *The History of the Abolition of the African Slave Trade,* which was published in 1808. His poet friend, William Wordsworth, read the manuscript for him before publication. Between 1823 and 1833 he was again active in helping to rouse the country in favor of the abolition of slavery in the British Empire.

The life of William Wilberforce (1759-1833) is of supreme importance for the social history of England. This man, later known as "Nightingale of the House of Commons" because of his lovely voice and superb speeches, was a small, feeble, round-shouldered man with poor digestion and eyesight. After a breakdown in 1788, he had to take minute doses of opium regularly for twenty years to maintain his health. In

The Scope of Evangelical Reform

spite of weak health, his affectionate nature, fine voice, gift of mimicry and rich mental endowment made him popular. Even after Wilberforce's conversion, William Pitt, who had been his friend in the easy social life of the day, remained his friend and did all he could to aid Wilberforce's struggle against the slave trade when he became Prime Minister.

Wilberforce spent some years at the Hull grammar school under the instruction of Isaac Milner, later famous as the evangelical leader at Cambridge. After his father died, when Wilberforce was nine, he was put under the care of an uncle who promised to make him his heir. His aunt was interested in Whitefield and imbued the boy with this evangelical spirit. When his mother heard of this, she took him home again to Hull. Here he entered into the gay social life of balls, theaters and cards, and the impressions of his uncle's home soon wore off. Perhaps a premonition of his later work was his letter as a boy of fourteen to the editor of a Yorkshire paper condemning the slave trade as an "odious traffic in human flesh."

In 1776 he went to St. John College at Cambridge where he formed a friendship with William Pitt. He was good in classical study, but the indulgence of his teachers left him deficient in mathematics. About this time the death of his uncle and grandfather left him with a fortune.

He decided on a parliamentary career and, after spending over £8,000 on the election, won a seat in the House of Commons where he represented Hull and later York. He joined all the London clubs and his fame as a mimic and singer as well as a conversationalist made him the darling of society.

But God was working in his life. When he won £600 one night from a man who could not afford to lose, he stopped card-playing. When Lord Camden refused to listen to his mimicry of others, Wilberforce gave that up. In the fall of 1784, after winning an election for a seat in York, he took a trip to the Continent with Isaac Milner. They read Philip Doddridge's book, *The Rise and Progress of Religion in the Soul*, together. On another trip the next year, at Milner's suggestion, they read the Greek New Testament to see if Doddridge's ideas were correct. Wilberforce was under deep spiritual conviction during 1785. He talked to John Newton several times, and decided that pride was his greatest sin. Late in 1785 he found spiritual relief and became an earnest Christian who gave up all his clubs and what he felt were activities not becoming a Christian. About this time he met Hannah More and her sisters. They became his spiritual helpers and he contributed £400 a year for several years to their Sunday school work.

His first interest was the formation of a society to stop the spread of vice. He got George III to issue a proclamation against immorality, and shortly after he founded the Proclamation Society. This was replaced in 1802 by the Society for the Suppression of Vice. He persuaded Prime Minister Perceval to reassemble Parliament so that the members need not travel on Sunday and persuaded the Speaker, Addington, to hold his social affairs on Saturday instead of Sunday.

As early as 1787 he wrote in his journal that God had set before him two objects, "the suppression of the slave trade and the reformation of manners." Several factors led him to this decision. He had talked with James Ramsay in 1783 concerning slavery. In 1786, Lady Middleton, who was shocked by Ramsay's descriptions of the slave trade in the West Indies, asked her husband Charles to bring it before Parliament. He did not feel that he was capable of such a task but wrote at his wife's urging to Wilberforce to ask him to lead the fight. Wilberforce replied that he felt unequal to the task but would call on them upon his return to London. In 1787 he met Clarkson and learned of the evils of the trade. His friend John Newton also told him of his firsthand experience of the slave trade. The convergence of all these forces and the urg-

The Scope of Evangelical Reform 71

ing of Pitt led him to undertake the leadership of the crusade in the House of Commons in 1787, the year in which the Anti-slavery Committee headed by Sharp was formed. Wilberforce did not join the Committee because it was thought that he would be more effective as an independent voice. He and other members of the Clapham Sect supported the African Association founded in 1788 to open up Africa for missionaries, trade and colonization.

The campaign began auspiciously with Prime Minister Pitt's open support. He ordered the Trade Committee of the Privy Council to report on the British trade in slaves from Africa. He also ordered William Eden, the British ambassador in Paris, to sound out the French government on the possibility of joint abolition by both countries. Clarkson at the same time began his tireless research to get facts to rouse the public. When Wilberforce became seriously ill in 1788, Pitt, after two interviews in which Clarkson gave him information concerning the slave trade, moved a resolution on May 9 binding the House to consider the slave trade in its next session. In this he was supported by the influential Fox and Burke. Thus the way was opened for the campaign in the House.

One member, Sir William Dolben, visited a slave ship. He was so horrified by what he saw that in June, 1788, he introduced a bill limiting the number of slaves that could be carried in a ship in proportion to its tonnage. This bill passed. The Abolition Committee had not been idle, for it held fifty-one meetings, gave out over 26,000 copies of reports on slavery and over 51,000 pamphlets. It also secured 301 petitions against slavery.

The report on slavery of the Trade Committee was published in April, 1789, and revealed the methods of slave capture, how slaves were carried to the West Indies, their treatment on the plantations, the extent of the trade and how other nations carried it on. On May 12, Wilberforce, who had somewhat recovered, in a long three-and-one-half hour speech in the House moved a resolution condemning slavery and asking for its abolition. A Select Committee, of which Wilberforce was a member, was ordered set up by the House so that the House could get its own evidence. This was a delaying action by the West Indian slave interests because the Privy Council Committee had already reported. Until the report was complete in 1791, Clarkson and Wilberforce worked long days collecting data.

It was well that Wilberforce got Wesley's last letter of encouragement in February, 1791, for the West Indian interests had adopted a policy of delay in order to block abolition. When he moved to bring in a bill for abolition that spring, his motion lost by a vote of 163 to 88.

The abolitionists, because it was plain that the House would not act, gave up the policy of securing favorable legislation by presenting evidence in Parliament of the evils of slavery. They began a campaign to arouse public opinion to force Parliament to act on abolition. Cowper wrote a poem, "The Negro's Complaint," which was set to music; Wedgwood sold lovely cameos with a picture of a Negro in chains pleading that he was also a man and a brother. A boycott of sugar grown on slavery plantations brought, according to Clarkson, 300,000 participants. Clarkson organized England, and a man named Dickson organized Scotland into districts to obtain petitions. England produced 312 and Scotland 187 anti-slavery petitions. Pro-slavery petitions numbered only five.

When Wilberforce moved for abolition in April, 1792, the motion again lost because England was fearful of the spread of the principles of the French Revolution which had become an international affair with the French declaration of war upon Austria. Clarkson's visit to France in 1789 had cast suspicion upon the abolitionists as Jacobins who favored a similar uprising in England. One gain was made as Wilberforce's motion was amended by Dundas to read that the House was in favor of "gradual abolition" of the trade. Though Dundas was opposed to Wilberforce and was helping those opposed to abolition, this was a small gain. The date for abolition was set for 1796. The Lords created further delay by deciding to hear evidence all over again in a Committee of the Whole. When England was plunged into war with France, any real action was long delayed, and the Abolition Committee did not even meet from 1796 to 1804.

Wilberforce did introduce a motion for abolition in 1796, the year when the bill of 1792 was to bring abolition into effect, but lost by a vote of 74 to 70 because about a dozen of the abolitionists had gone to an opera, *The Two Hunchbacks*, by Gobbio. He was confirmed in his dislike of the theater by this incident.

During the next year he published his book, *A Practical View of Christianity*. It sold widely and was translated into several languages. In it he contrasted real evangelical Christianity with the cold ethical Christianity practiced by the upper classes. His life was further enriched in this year by his marriage. He demonstrated his patriotism by giving one-eighth of his net income voluntarily to the government. In 1797 he gave £2,000 to charity and before marriage gave away each year one-quarter of his income.

In 1802 the abolitionists put out the first issue of the *Christian Observer*, an anti-slavery magazine which was edited by Zachary Macaulay for a time. Clarkson had also recovered his health enough to be back at work. On May 30, 1804, Wilberforce introduced a bill for abolition with the support of Pitt, Fox and the new Irish representatives who had been added to the English Parliament by an act of 1800. The bill passed and was sent to the House of Lords where it was delayed until 1805. The final bill, introduced on January 2, 1807, provided that the trade in slaves would end on January 1, 1808, and stated that a £100 fine would be assessed for each slave carried, and that the slave ship would be forfeited to the Crown. By 1806 the bill passed in the House and in 1807 in the House of Lords. In 1811 an amending act made slave trading a felony to be punished by transportation to a penal colony. After the bill passed in the House, Wilberforce jubilantly asked Henry Thornton what they should abolish next, and Thornton suggested that they might attack the lottery.

Englishmen could no longer engage legally in the slave trade, but the "Saints" did not relax their caution. They created the African Institution in 1807 with the Duke of Gloucester as president in order to see that the act was enforced, to get other countries to abolish the trade and to encourage the civilization of Africa. Zachary Macaulay's advice led to the provision of naval vessels to intercept illegal slave ships, to the setting up of Admiralty Courts to decide the fate of such ships and to orders to take slaves found on such ships to a colony, to put them in the army or to take them to their homes, according to their wishes. The squadron cost the country £750,000 a year and rescued over 3,000 slaves a year. In all, patrols cost England about £15,000,000 between 1815 and 1839. From 1840 on, it is estimated that about one-sixth of the navy was engaged in this work with a loss of 5 per cent of the personnel due to fever and heat off the African coast.

The slave trade had become illegal for the British. Next the "Saints" took on the task of getting it banned for Europeans by a general statement of the powers at the forthcoming Congress of Vienna at the end of the Napoleonic wars. Their activities in this connection showed what an aroused Christian conscience can do even in influencing international meetings. Wilberforce in a letter to Gisbourne, a member of the Clapham Sect, wrote that it would be "a great and blessed close" to their work if they could get the great European powers to agree to a statement for the general abolition of the slave trade. In pursuing this end, he had talks with Alexander I of Russia and also won the esteem of the Prussian king to the extent that he sent him a set of Dresden china. The "Saints" were heartened by the abolition of the trade in Denmark in 1804, in the United States in 1808, in Sweden in 1813 and in Holland in 1814.

Lord Castlereagh, then Foreign Secretary, returned from negotiations with France which led to the first Peace of Paris in the spring of 1814. This peace allowed the French slave trade to continue for some time. Wilberforce made a speech in the House in which he said that Castlereagh had, in this treaty, the death warrant for many slaves in the hands of the French traders. Castlereagh, who at first looked on the abolitionists as left-wing radicals or at best sentimental idealists, later came to the conclusion that the slave trade was immoral. The abolitionists secured nearly 800 petitions with about one million names, asking the government to take strong action to end the French slave trade. In the House of Commons strong resolutions were passed asking the government to secure "the immediate and universal abolition of the slave trade" by European powers.

When Napoleon returned from Elba for his final 100 days' campaign against the powers of Europe in 1815, he ended the French slave trade. After Napoleon's defeat Louis XVIII confirmed this action, but the French trade was not finally stopped until 1831. In 1815, eight powers at Vienna signed a joint declaration, which became a part of the final act of the Congress, to the effect that the trade should be condemned and that universal abolition was worthy of attention, and promised to use all efforts to bring it about soon. This principle, however, had to be put into effect by direct negotiations between England and each one of the slave-trading countries. To obtain a treaty with Portugal abolishing slavery, England in 1815 remitted a debt of £450,000 which Portugal owed to England and gave her a gift of £300,000 to compensate her for Portuguese ships siezed in the slave trade. A similar treaty with Spain in 1817 was obtained at the cost of a gift of £400,000. Not until 1820 and 1830, however, did Portugal and Spain fully carry out these treaties.

Wilberforce also warmly supported the revolting Spanish colonies in Latin America because, if freed, he thought they would discourage the slave trade and abolish slavery. By 1823, when the abolitionists took up the total abolition of slavery itself, the Clapham Sect, supported by a strong Christian public opinion, had succeeded in the abolition of the slave trade formerly carried on by European nations. In a letter to Babington in 1821, Wilberforce stated that his greatest blessings had come in being the instrument under God of the abolition of the slave trade and of opening India to missions.

3. *The Amelioration of Slavery,* 1808-1823

Before adopting the principle of complete abolition of slavery in 1823, the "Saints" tried to bring about an amelioration of the conditions of slaves, especially in the British West Indies. Their instruments were ordinances of the Colonial Office and the threat of parliamentary legislation, which brought pressure to bear upon the colonial legislatures. Sir James Stephen, son of the James Stephen of the Clapham Sect, drafted most of the ameliorative ordinances. Educated for law and called to the bar in 1813, he was appointed as legal advisor to the Colonial Office, and rose in that Office until he became Assistant Undersecretary in 1834 and Undersecretary in 1847. The colonial legislatures refused to cooperate with measures for amelioration because they were composed mainly of slave owners who resented English pressure upon their local assemblies.

In order to prevent the importation of more slaves and to protect those on the plantations, an order-in-council in 1812 ordered the registration of slaves. The African Institution

The Scope of Evangelical Reform

in 1815 put out a pamphlet stating the reasons for registration. In 1819, an act, largely Stephen's work, was passed which required duplicate registers of slaves to be kept in the colonies and in London. No slave could be sold or mortgaged without such registration. The intransigence of the colonial legislatures between 1815 and 1823 finally brought the Clapham Sect to the position that slavery itself must be abolished. Amelioration was not workable because the colonial legislatures would not co-operate. After 1823, from a policy of gradual abolition they moved to one of immediate abolition of slavery in 1833, the year in which the final act abolishing slavery in British possessions was passed. They faced the dilemma of colonial property rights in slaves which should not be damaged, and colonial attempts to claim more power than the imperial government.

4. *Abolition of Slavery in the British Empire,* 1823-1833

While Wilberforce and Clarkson were active in the campaign for abolition of slavery in this period, they were both too old to carry on as formerly. Clarkson's role as an expert researcher and propagandist was assumed by Zachary Macaulay. And, at the request of Wilberforce, T. Fowell Buxton assumed the mantle of leadership of the abolitionist forces in the House of Commons. Wilberforce lost his wealth through an unwise investment in his son William's farming venture and lived his last years in the homes of his clergymen-sons, Robert and Samuel. Before his death in 1833 he was able to thank God that abolition had become a reality.

Since Zachary Macaulay (1768-1838) came from a large Scottish family of twelve children, his minister-father found it impossible to give him a college education. He went to a merchant's office in Glasgow at the age of fourteen for two years. Here he met university students who destroyed his faith and led him into a profligate life. Between 1784 and 1789 he was a bookkeeper and manager of an estate in Jamaica where he saw the evils of slavery and became hardened to them. A position in England in the business of one of his uncles was offered to him in 1792. His brother-in-law, Thomas Babington, took the raw uncouth lad in hand and helped him not only to become socially polished but led him to Christ and introduced him to the Clapham Sect.

Between 1794 and 1799 he served as governor of Sierra Leone with distinction and was able to meet the problems of discontent of the settlers and the wreck of the settlement in 1794 by the French. Ill with fever, he was ordered home by the directors of the company in 1795. Ill though he was, rather than take a passenger ship directly to England, he took passage in a slave ship to Barbados. His work in Jamaica had acquainted him with plantation slavery, and his stay in Sierra Leone had let him see the slave trade in Africa. This trip to Barbados revealed to him the horrors of slave ships.

Rather surprisingly, he had to face the opposition of the godly More sisters to his marriage to their pupil, Selina Mills, whom they could not bear to give up. His marriage was made possible later by a position as secretary of the Sierra Leone company at £400 a year.

Between 1802 and 1816 he served as editor of the *Christian Observer* and not only helped to found the African Institution (organized to seek enforcement of the ban on slave trade) but served as its unpaid secretary from 1807 to 1812. By 1818 his trading company in India and West Africa had prospered until he was worth £100,000. When he was asked to help Buxton in the fight to abolish slavery in 1823, he moved into a less expensive office. He also deliberately limited his connection with the firm to have time for antislavery work and left its management to a nephew, Thomas Babington, whose poor management led to the company's financial ruin in Macaulay's declining years. Such was the extent of Macaulay's consecration to the cause of the slave and to Christ.

The Scope of Evangelical Reform 79

In 1823 the Anti-Slavery Society was formed to abolish slavery and in 1825 the *Anti-Slavery Reporter,* with Macaulay as editor, was started. The periodical presented facts in favor of the abolition of slavery and refuted arguments advanced by opponents.

Macaulay became the researcher for Buxton and his supporters and his knowledge both of slavery and the slave trade helped him to get facts. He was a good statistician, had an encyclopedic memory and was accurate and fair. When information was needed on slavery, Wilberforce would jokingly say, "Look it up in Macaulay." Between 1799 and 1833 his investigations covered the whole field of West Indian slavery and marshaled evidence that was unanswerable. He was one of the first to see that the abolition of the slave trade must be followed by the abolition of slavery.

While Macaulay worked behind the scenes as Clarkson had done earlier, Buxton replaced Wilberforce as the parliamentary leader of the abolitionists. T. Fowell Buxton (1786-1845), the son of the High Sheriff of Essex, was nicknamed "Elephant Buxton" by his classmates because of his 6'4" height. After his father's death, his Quakeress mother instilled in him a love for the Bible, an ethical life and a detestation of slavery. For several years he stayed home and engaged in field sports until a visit in 1801 to the Gurney home imbued him with a desire to learn. In this home he met Elizabeth, later a prison reformer, and his future wife, Hannah Gurney. He went to the University of Dublin where he won highest academic honors including a gold medal. He was asked to be a candidate to represent the University of Dublin in Parliament, but declined. One of his uncles opened up the way for him to work in a large brewery in 1808. He soon proved his ability as a businessman and made a large fortune over the years. While he worked hard at business, he studied English literature and political economy on the side.

Serious study of the Scriptures after 1806 led him to a

deeper interest in religion and in 1811 he was able to lead a dying brother to Christ. Through the preaching of Josiah Pratt and a severe illness in 1813, he was led into a mature experience of salvation by faith in Christ alone. He ever remained thankful for this illness. He became earnest in private and family prayer and desired to know the will of God.

He became active in philanthropic works on behalf of the poor. During the hard winter of 1816 he gave money to establish a free soup kitchen for the poor weavers of Spitalfields and raised over £43,000 for their relief by a speech in the Mansion House. The work of his sister-in-law, Elizabeth Fry, in Newgate Prison interested him in prison reform between 1818 and 1822. He helped to form a Society for the Reformation of Prison Discipline in 1816. On January 15, 1817, in a letter to his wife he showed the direction of his consecration by writing that more of himself—time, influence and affections—must be devoted to "the honor of God and the happiness of men." In 1818, he published a book on the subject of whether crime was produced or prevented by the system of prison discipline then used. He won an election in 1818 to represent Weymouth in the House of Commons and was put on a committee checking prisons and the criminal code. As a result, in 1821 legislation was passed to reform prisons.

By 1819, a letter to a friend indicated that the slave trade was becoming as important in his thinking as the condition of the poor, prisons and criminal law. His sister-in-law, Priscilla Gurney, who was dying of consumption, moved into his home in 1820 and her last wish before dying in 1822 was that he might help "the poor dear slaves." On May 24, 1821, Wilberforce wrote to Buxton concerning slaves in the Empire and stated that he was looking for an eligible leader in this holy enterprise. He asked Buxton to consider the wisdom of devoting himself to the "blessed service" of freeing the slaves by law. While he did not make up his mind until later to assume leadership which Wilberforce was dropping, the crusade for the abolition of slavery was his main interest after 1822. He made a thorough study of slavery for a year and a half after Wilberforce's letter. When Wilberforce and Macaulay visited him at his home in the fall of 1822, he made Wilberforce rejoice by agreeing to become his "associate and successor." In a letter dated March 22, 1823, he wrote to his wife that he was "very earnest about slavery" and thought that it was to be "the main business of my life."

In January 1823 an Anti-Slavery Society was organized, and two years later Macaulay began and edited the *Anti-Slavery Reporter* to inform the public concerning the evils of slavery and the need for emancipation. It sold as many as 20,000 copies a month.

The attack opened on May 15, 1823, when Buxton moved a resolution in the House of Commons stating that slavery was repugnant to the British constitution and the Christian religion and "ought to be abolished gradually throughout the British colonies." In his speech he said that the "extinction of slavery" in all British possessions was the aim of the abolitionists. An opponent was able to get the motion amended so that it called for "amelioration" of the condition of slaves rather than "abolition" of slavery.

From 1823 the government tried without much success to get the West Indian legislatures to pass slave codes to ameliorate the condition of slaves. In Demerara, British Guiana, news of the debate was withheld by the local authorities from the slaves, who rebelled, thinking the British government had freed them and their masters were keeping them in slavery illegally. The revolt was ruthlessly repressed, and terrible punishments, such as 1000 lashes at one time, were actually inflicted on one slave. William Smith, a Methodist missionary, was blamed falsely for the uprising and condemned to death but died in prison. This uprising was blamed on the abolitionists, and the colonial legislatures became more antagonistic than ever to the English government's policy of amelioration.

But the abolitionists had not been idle. In 1823 the aged Clarkson had traveled 3,000 miles and had been away from home a year organizing nearly 200 anti-slavery committees and obtaining over 100 petitions advocating abolition. He also wrote a pamphlet to show that abolition would not ruin England economically. By March, 1824, nearly 600 petitions were secured. Two years later Buxton presented a petition from London bearing 72,000 names of persons advocating abolition. He set the pattern for the act of 1833 by a speech in 1824 advocating "compensation" for the slave owner and "emancipation" for the children of slaves. In this way slavery would be gradually abolished. James Stephen, Sr., also wrote a two-volume work on slavery in the West Indies.

The Mauritius scandal, beginning in 1825 and revealed to Parliament by Buxton in May, 1826, discredited the slave owners and created an anti-slavery public opinion. Buxton with the help of witnesses from the island and Macaulay's excellent organization of data was able to show that the slave trade continued there after its abolition and that it would have been necessary for every slave woman to have 180 children to account for the number of slaves owned between 1810 and 1825 if they had not been illegally imported in violation of the act of 1807. The evidence was so overwhelming that in 1827 it brought on an attack of apoplexy in Buxton. While recuperating, he greatly influenced along humanitarian lines William Bentinck, later governor of India. This impact led Bentinck to abolish *suttee*, the burning of Hindu widows on their husbands' funeral pyres. He also helped John Philip in 1828 to secure legislation establishing the civil rights of the colored people in Cape Colony.

The delay in exposing the Mauritius scandal in the House was caused by the death of the governor of the island and Buxton's illness, but an unofficial inquiry by Buxton proved that there were illegal imports and the government in 1830 ordered the emancipation of nearly all the slaves there on the ground that they had been illegally acquired. This scandal convinced the abolitionists that the policy of amelioration and an evolutionary progress to emancipation, followed since 1823, would never work. In May, 1830, in a meeting in Freemasons Hall in London, Buxton, with Wilberforce in the chair, moved for the entire abolition of slavery throughout the British dominions at the earliest moment.

The abolitionists lost the services of Macaulay whose health broke in April and whose wife died in May of 1831. His early experience of slavery in Jamaica, and his contact with the trade in Sierra Leone coupled with his ability as a researcher and propagandist had made him an indispensable aid to the abolitionists both in the movements to abolish the trade and slavery. He had lost his fortune because of his consecration to the abolitionist cause but made no complaints.

The more radical abolitionists became impatient after 1830 and, under the leadership of George Stephen (1794-1879), a son of James Stephen, Sr., in 1831 they organized "The Agency Committee" to arrange for anti-slavery public meetings and to promote petitions to Parliament to end slavery. The Committee had six paid lecturers touring England in this work. On April 15, 1831, Buxton presented 500 anti-slavery petitions and moved a resolution for the abolition of slavery. On January 1, 1832, Buxton recorded his prayer that God would bless his work in the extinction of slavery or rather would "take the work into thine own hands." Upon motion in May, 1832, by Buxton, committees of Lords and of the House of Commons were set up which decided that slavery was so evil that abolition was the only cure and that it could be carried out safely. Buxton called upon the churches of England to set aside January 16, 1833, as a national day of prayer for the abolition of slavery. On March 19 he gave notice he would enter a motion for abolition on April 23, 1833. On May 14 he presented petitions with 187,000 names secured in ten days by several ladies. Petitions with over 20,000 names from Edinburgh and 31,000 names from Glasgow were also presented.

James Stephen, Jr., in the Colonial Office was asked to draw up a bill quickly over a weekend. Although he kept Sunday strictly, he relaxed his principles on behalf of the slaves and from Saturday noon to Monday noon drew up the long bill necessary. This bill and the Colonial Office ordinances asking the colonies to set up slave registers were his work. The bill was introduced by Colonial Secretary Stanley on May 14 and became law on August 28, 1833, after the King signed it.

The law freed all slaves six years of age and under, agricultural field slaves were freed but required to serve an apprenticeship of six years, while domestic slaves were freed and required to serve a four-year apprenticeship. The sum of £20,000,000 was set aside to compensate the owners of slaves. On August 1, 1834, the bill went into effect and about 700,000 slaves in British colonies were freed because of this Christian crusade. Wilberforce died on July 29, thanking God that he could live to see the day in which England would allot "twenty millions sterling for the abolition of slavery." In a speech to the London Missionary Society in May of 1833, Buxton, while acknowledging the debt of slaves to Wilberforce and Macaulay, said that the Christian people of England were the instrument and God was the Author of abolition.

The five Commissioners to decide claims for compensation, of whom James Stephen, Jr., was one, estimated that there were 780,993 slaves valued at £45,281,738. By 1841, £15,125,347 had been paid on 39,790 claims and, by 1845, the £20,000,000 had been paid out at a cost of £150,000. Of the

The Scope of Evangelical Reform 85

total, £16,589,373 went for 670,000 slaves in the West Indies, and South African slave owners got £1,247,401 for 35,475 slaves.

The famous British historian, George M. Trevelyan, wrote that if the slave trade and slavery had not been brought to an end by the Christian conscience of England aroused by the abolitionists, the Industrial Revolution would have made Africa a great slave farm in the twentieth century and slavery would have wrecked civilization in Europe, Africa and North America.[1] Abolitionism was to him a turning-point in the world's history. Elié Halévy was of the opinion that abolition was "first and foremost a Christian movement" although political liberalism did co-operate with the Evangelicals in the passage of legislation.[2]

The fight was not completely won, because Buxton and his followers had to watch over the apprentices whose apprenticeship would not end for field laborers until 1841 and for domestic laborers until 1838. In March, 1836, Buxton moved a resolution for a committee to see how apprenticeship was working, and a committee was appointed with him as a member. Evidence in publications by Joseph Sturge and others who visited the West Indies in 1836 led to the decision to end the apprenticeship system on August 1, 1838, and to give complete freedom to the ex-slave. It is interesting to note that exports from the British West Indies to England went up from £2,575,000 to £3,450,000 between 1834 and 1838 after the slaves were freed. The colored potential or actual sons of God had become physically free and did better work as a result.

---

[1] George Macaulay Trevelyan, *A Shortened History of England* (Toronto: Longmans, Green & Co., 1942), p. 423.

[2] Elié Halévy, *A History of the English People, 1830-1841* (New York: Harcourt, Brace & Co., n.d.), pp. 85, 86.

5. The Protection of Colored People after 1834

Buxton and his friends, after freeing the slaves, did not leave the colored peoples to their fate but became interested in the treatment of aborigines in all the British possessions. In the session of the House in 1835 he was able to carry a resolution for the appointment of a committee to report on the treatment of the natives in the Kaffir war in Africa, and he became the chairman of the Committee. He wrote in January, 1834: "My object is to inquire into past proceedings, for the purpose of instituting certain rules and laws, on principles of justice, for the future treatment of the aborigines of those countries where we make settlements."[3] He told his constituency in the 1835 election that the completion of emancipation, the abolition of the Portuguese and the Spanish slave trade and the just treatment of the aborigines were his main interest.

The committee originally appointed in 1835 to inquire into the Kaffir war in South Africa widened its scope to include consideration of the treatment of the aborigines in all British lands after its reappointment in 1835. The missionary, John Philip, gave evidence before it. When all the evidence was in, Buxton as chairman faced the task of drawing up the committee report. He wanted it to become a manual for the future treatment of the aborigines in the colonies and enlisted the aid of John Philip in drawing up the final report.

The report of 1837 contrasted the destructively cruel treatment which the natives received in some colonies with the increase in population, civilization and Christianity in those where the natives were well-treated. It recommended that the natives should be under the protection of the executive of the colony who was responsible to the British government rather than under the locally elected colonial legislature; that con-

---

[3]Charles Buxton, ed., *Memoirs of Sir Thomas Fowell Buxton, Bart.* (London: John Murray, 2nd ed., 1849), p. 369.

tracts for service by natives be strictly regulated to keep them from becoming forced laborers or slaves; that no liquor be sold to aborigines; that native lands be sold to whites only through and by the executive in order to protect native rights in the land; that consideration be given to the religious development of the natives; that only the British and not the local government could make treaties with the native chief; and that the governments should protect missionary efforts in the colonies. Buxton did all this while he was at the same time chairman of the committee on the treatment of apprentices. The *Cambridge History of the British Empire*[4] describes the report of the committee as a step on the road that led to the mandate system of the League of Nations and the trusteeship principle adopted by the United Nations. Buxton believed that the more civilized lands should accept the principle of trusteeship under God for colored people with less advanced cultures. James Stephen in the Colonial Office put these principles into effect as far as he could.

Just after he presented his report in 1837, Buxton was defeated for re-election in Weymouth because he refused to open the "pubs" and "lend" (really bribes) £1,000 to the voters. In 1837 he founded the Aborigines Protection Society, and in 1839 the British and Foreign Anti-Slavery Society to protect the natives and to stamp out the final remnants of the slave trade. These two societies were merged in 1909 to form the Anti-slavery and Aborigines Protection Society. From this it will be seen that Buxton turned from emancipation when that was completed to the work of protecting natives in the colonies and to bringing about the acceptance by the British public of the concept of trusteeship for the natives in the colonies.

John Philip (1775-1851), a Scotchman with a powerful

---

[4] John Holland Rose, Arthur Percival Newton, Ernest Alfred Benians, eds., *The Cambridge History of the British Empire* (Cambridge: Cambridge University Press, 1940, Vol. II), p. 661.

physique and keen piercing eyes, was an excellent orator and conversationalist. He was born into a weaver's family, and became a master-weaver with other weavers working under him by the time he was twenty-one. A religious conversion in the revival during the 1790's led him into the Congregational ministry after three years of preparation. He began his ministry in 1792 and in 1804 became the pastor of a large Congregational church in Aberdeen. His missionary messages led several of his congregation to volunteer as missionaries. Columbia College (now Columbia University) in 1819, and the College of New Jersey (now Princeton University) in 1820, each awarded him an honorary Doctor of Divinity degree because of his theological and missionary endeavors.

He was asked by the London Missionary Society in 1817 to go to South Africa in order to become superintendent of the Society's missions. He arrived in 1819 and soon grasped the situation in Cape Colony. He saw that the missionary concept of equality of the races under God was in conflict with the concept which the Boers, the descendants of the Dutch settlers, held. They believed that the natives were inferior to the white man.

Philip was determined to prevent the degradation of the Cape colored people, the descendants of the Hottentots and whites, into a slave people. He wanted for them civil equality with the whites and the right to hold land legally. Philip in 1822 wrote to Brenton, a friend in England, to interview Wilberforce and Buxton and enlist their support on behalf of the Hottentots. Wilberforce, in July in the House, asked the government to consider the state of the Hottentots. Later action by the House of Commons set up a commission to inquire into the condition of the Hottentots. It took evidence in South Africa in 1823, but in spite of Buxton's efforts the report of the commission was not given to the House until 1830. The report verified Philip's charges that the Hottentots were forced to labor on public works, prevented from entering missionary institutions and refused the right to hold land.

Philip realized by 1825 that nothing could be expected from the report of the commission and after a tour to gather information returned to England, early in 1826. Here he successfully cultivated the friendship of Buxton and Wilberforce. Advised to do so by Zachary Macaulay, Philip decided to appeal to British public opinion through a book, the two-volume *Researches in South Africa,* which he published in April, 1828. Though there were some errors of fact in the work, the mass of testimony which he advanced supported his main contention that the condition of the Hottentots needed improving. This could only be done through extending to them the protection of the British government. He showed that they had originally had lands and cattle, but both they and the missionaries had to face increasing limitations from the local and colonial administration. If they were granted civil rights and land, he thought they could become independent producers and consumers.

The threat of the possible effect of the *Researches* on public opinion strengthened Buxton's hand in Parliament. The Colonial Secretary Murray promised Buxton that if he would make no motions the Government would act. On July 15, 1828, Buxton moved an address to the Crown asking that the Colonial government at Capetown be instructed to give the same liberties to the Hottentots which other settlers enjoyed.

Meanwhile, in South Africa news of Philip's appeal to the British public and the humanitarianism of the new governor, Bourke, led to the promulgation by the Governor, on July 17, 1828, of Ordinance Fifty. Philip insisted that this ordinance would be useless unless the British government issued an order-in-council to validate it. This order was sent on January 15, 1829. The Ordinance exempted natives from the requirement that they must have passes from the authorities if they left their own district, gave them custody of their children, control of their own labor and the right to hold land. This was the Magna Charta of liberty for the Cape colored people. It came through the combined efforts of Philip and Buxton to get the British government to protect the aborigines along the lines laid down in Buxton's later report on the Treatment of the aborigines. Once again Christian idealism had forced favorable political action on behalf of those unable to protect themselves.

About this time Buxton became interested in commerce as a better means to combat the continuing remnants of the slave trade than the patrol system by which British ships had tried to stop the export of slaves from Africa. The patrols had cost the government about £15,000,000 between 1815 and 1839, but slavery still continued surreptitiously. He published *The African Slave Trade and Its Remedy* in two parts, in 1839 and 1840. In it he depicted the evils of the trade and how legitimate commerce on the West Africa coast might more quickly bring it to an end. African products could be exchanged for European goods in legitimate trade so the native chiefs would not need to sell their people for European products. In June, 1839, in Exeter Hall, with the Prince Consort, Albert, as patron, he formed the Society for the Extinction of the Slave Trade and the Civilization of Africa. He drew up a long memorandum setting forth his idea which he presented to the Cabinet for favorable action.

Buxton believed that treaties with native chiefs and commerce and civilization must supplement the patrols. The Bible and the plow must go hand in hand. He proposed an expedition up the Niger to make treaties with the native chiefs and to find sites for trading stations to open up the way for commerce and missions. The Cabinet accepted his theory and £60,000 was voted for the expedition. Buxton believed that Africa would be delivered from slavery by "calling forth her own resources" through Christianity, education, agriculture and commerce. On March 9, 1839, he wrote that "the

The Scope of Evangelical Reform 91

project of overturning the slave trade by civilization, Christianity and the cultivation of the soil . . ." was now in the hands of the government.

Three ships sailed in the spring of 1841 to explore the Niger and the resources along its banks, to make treaties with the native chieftains, to end the slave trade and to open the way for peaceful trade. The expedition failed because of fever which attacked its personnel. Forty-one of 193 Europeans died of fever, but not one of 108 Africans of the expedition died. The news of the failure of his project weakened Buxton's already feeble health. This failure should not blind us to the accomplishments through emancipation in 1834, the Aborigines Report and the founding of the Aborigines Protection Society, of this Bible-reading and praying Christian who put his faith into practice.

Missionary executives and missionaries as well as statesmen were convinced that the church should support and promote lawful trade with the natives of Africa as a means to kill the slave trade and to advance the cause of Christianity and civilization. Henry Venn, for many years secretary of the Church Missionary Society, believed that trade would promote the independence of the native Christian and more effectively end the slave trade than the African patrols. Palmerston, the head of government and father-in-law of Shaftesbury, favored treaties with the chiefs to open up legitimate trade.

Livingstone was one of the foremost supporters of the idea that legitimate trade would drive out the slave trader and support the conversion and civilization of the African. When he met Philip in South Africa, he was pleased with Philip's idea that the natives could, by becoming producers of raw materials and consumers of European goods, become independent and civilized Christians. This idea caused conflict between him and the Boers on his first mission station. His discovery of the Zambezi and first personal contact with the

Arab slave trade in 1851 led him to develop the idea that, if the natives could trade raw materials for European products, they would not need to sell their people as slaves. In a letter to the home office in London in October of that year, he advocated trade "for legitimate" purposes as a means to end the slave trade. English goods exchanged for African raw materials would make the slave trade unnecessary. He proposed that the mission support such a policy. Mammon could be called into the service of God; commerce and Christianity in alliance could civilize Africa. His trips to the west and east coasts of Africa between 1853 and 1856 were for the purpose of opening up a road for legitimate trade with the interior.

Upon his return to England in 1856, after his transcontinental crossing of Africa, he pushed this idea wherever possible. When he was awarded the Patron's Gold Medal by the Royal Geographical Society, he emphasized that trade in raw materials, such as cotton, chinchona and cane, for European manufactured goods would supplement the work of the cruiser patrols in ending the Arab and Portuguese slave trade of East Africa. In a letter printed in the December 29, 1856, issue of *The Times* of London, he urged the native growing of cotton as a way to open trade with Central Africa. He looked upon his explorations as "the beginning of the missionary enterprise" and legitimate commerce. His book, *Missionary Travels and Researches in South Africa,* published in 1857, had the same emphasis. In a speech to the combined meetings of the Manchester Chamber of Commerce, the Commercial Association, and the Cotton Supply Association of Manchester on September 9, 1857, he spoke glowingly of the capacity of central Africa to produce raw cotton in exchange for European products. In a speech in December, 1857, given in the Senate House of Cambridge University just before his return to Africa to head a government expedition up the Zambezi, he said that he was returning to Africa to open a path in order that "civilization, commerce and Christianity" might enter there. Such were his firm convictions, and his later endeavors were to open a path for trade as well as missions. This was to be a means to the grand end—the winning of the native to the Christian faith.

James Stewart, a missionary in the industrial mission school for natives at Lovedale, South Africa, and a cousin of James Stewart, the road builder of Nyasaland, in a letter to the Livingstonia Missionary Committee in Scotland in 1878, urged that a company be founded to trade with the natives of that area. James Stevenson, the Scotch businessman who financed the Stevenson Road between Lakes Nyasa and Tanganyika, took up the idea with the Glasgow Chamber of Commerce in November, 1876. By June, 1878, the Livingstonia Central African Trading Company was chartered, with Stevenson as chairman. The company would buy ivory in the interior and carry it to the coast in steamers. Before slaves had been used to carry the ivory and were sold with it at the coast. Three coffee plants from the Edinburgh Botanical Gardens were sent out to John Duncan, a missionary. One plant lived and, through the efforts of John Buchanan, became the nucleus of a flourishing coffee production. Along with ivory, cotton and oil seeds, it became the basis of profitable legitimate trade. The company also engaged actively in the campaign to end the trade in slaves and supported the missions of the Scottish churches in Central Africa. The company had £20,000 of capital in shares each worth £500 and paid its first dividend of two and one-half per cent by its eighth year. In 1889 all the assets of the company were sold to Cecil Rhodes' British South Africa Company. The company helped to suppress the Arab slave trade and helped missionaries and settlers to get into the interior.

In all these endeavors to further legitimate trade, it will be noticed that trade was a means to the suppression of the slave trade and the spread of Christianity and civilization in

Africa. There can be no question on the basis of an examination of the sources of the Christian sincerity of men like Livingstone and Stevenson. That they might make a profit was secondary to the major objective.

6. *Treaty States and Protectorates*

John Philip's attention, after securing Ordinance Fifty in 1828, was increasingly directed toward the problem of how to protect the native tribes on the frontier of white settlement from slavery and exploitation by the white traders and settlers. The Griquas in the north and the Kaffirs to the east of Cape Colony desired to hold their lands while the Boers wanted to take their lands and to stop cattle thefts by the natives. Philip proposed that the British government sign treaties of alliance with these native chieftains. A British adviser would reside within the tribe. Except for the agent and missionaries, all Europeans were to be kept out of the tribe. The chiefs would keep order on the frontier and be paid for this work.

This policy was first applied to the Griqua tribe, the offspring of European settlers and native women, about 1,800, on the northern frontier of Cape Colony. They had migrated 800 miles north of Capetown. In 1813, Campbell had persuaded them to adopt the name Griqua and to call their town Griquatown. The best road to the interior ran through their lands and was coveted by the Boers and European traders. In 1833, Philip urged that his treaty state system be used to protect the Griqua. Governor D'Urban of Cape Colony in 1834 at the urging of Philip signed the first such treaty with the Griqua chief Waterboer. Waterboer was to keep order in his lands and protect the frontier. He was to be paid an annual salary in muskets and cash with a £50 grant for missions. A missionary was appointed as the British agent. By 1843, a treaty was also negotiated with another Griqua chief, Adam Kok. This prevented Boer expansion to the north and gave the missionaries the opportunity to evangelize and civilize the Griqua.

The Boers, stopped from expanding to the north by this policy, moved eastward where they came into conflict with the Kaffirs. A war between the Kaffirs and the Boers in 1834 involved Cape Colony and in 1836, led in England to the appointment of the Aborigines Committee in the House of Commons under the chairmanship of Buxton. Because compensation paid for slaves after they were freed in 1834 did not equal the value of the slaves and because of the missionaries' protection of the natives, the Boers began the Great Trek out of Cape Colony in 1836. This trek resulted in the founding of the Boer Republics of the Orange Free State and Transvaal.

Pressure by the Boers and the expense involved led the British government to give up Philip's treaty state policy and to leave the natives to the mercies of the colonial government. A policy of annexation of the native areas to the crown replaced the treaty state policy of Philip which had protected the natives from unscrupulous raiders and land grabbers. Philip had used the policy as a means to an end, the protection of the natives, until missionaries could civilize and convert them. This policy was to be used by missionaries elsewhere as a means by which natives would be protected by the more humane British government under the influence of a strong Christian public opinion.

Although Philip's treaty state policy was unsuccessful in South Africa, a similar policy advocated by missionaries and the humanitarians in England had better results in New Zealand. An evangelical Anglican, Samuel Marsden (1764-1838), was made chaplain in 1793 of the convict settlement of New South Wales. Here he met the Maori natives of New Zealand who served in ships that called at Sydney. He noticed how virile and intelligent they were. His request to the Church Missionary Society led to the sending out of a carpenter and a shoemaker to civilize and convert the Maori. In 1814 he took them to New Zealand, got a grant of 200 acres of land by deed from the native chief for a missionary station. He brought a clergyman to supplement the lay efforts of these men in 1819 and secured a larger block of land. The Maori language was written down and the Bible put into the native tongue. Later on Marsden persuaded the Methodists also to send missionaries.

Tribal war after 1830, the debasing influence of the whalers who called there when whaling in those areas and the greed of settlers for land made difficulty for the natives and for missionaries, who by 1838 had seventy-one Christian Maori communicants. A land company, the New Zealand Association, was formed in England in 1837 to settle the area. James Stephen in the Colonial Office blocked the efforts of the Association to get a charter because he feared it would lead to the "conquest and extermination" of the Maoris.

Captain William Hobson was sent out by the English government to negotiate a treaty with the Maoris. Missionary support helped him to secure the treaty, and the ideas of James Stephen, Jr., to protect the natives were incorporated into the Treaty of Waitangi which Hobson signed with the Maori chiefs in 1840. The chiefs gave up sovereignty to the British government in return for complete possession of their lands, which could only be sold to the British colonial government rather than directly to settlers and land companies. Fear that the French might annex New Zealand had speeded this decision, but it is doubtful whether the Maori chiefs would have been so willing to sign if the missionary Henry Williams had not been Hobson's interpreter and had not urged signature upon the chiefs. New Zealand became a part of British possessions with safeguards for the natives. In no other area of the world have relations between the natives and white population been so successful. Marsden's statesman-

The Scope of Evangelical Reform 97

ship and the fine missionary work of Williams made this advance possible.

Missionary influence and appeals to the British Government through Christian public opinion were largely responsible for the annexation of Bechuanaland in South Africa in 1885 as a protectorate. Under a protectorate, the chiefs controlled their people under native law but dealt with the outside world through a British resident or agent. Bechuanaland had been the scene of Moffat's labors in giving the people the Bible in their own Sechuana language, and Livingstone saw that this area where he began his missionary work was the key to the road to the north. This road would be closed to missions if the Boers were to get control of the area.

John MacKenzie worked among the natives in the area from 1858 until his death except for a period of service under the government. He held that the proper and first objective of all missionary effort was evangelism to win the natives to Christ. After that they were to be trained in the Christian life and given the arts of civilization. In order to carry this out he labored at a later date to forestall the Boer's annexation of his beloved Bechuanaland and was largely responsible for the British protectorate over Bechuanaland in 1885.

Trouble developed in the area because the Boer republics wished to block the British advance to the north from Cape Colony. Cecil Rhodes was interested in a Cape-to-Cairo railroad to link a belt of British possessions from Capetown to Cairo. Rhodes wanted Bechuanaland annexed to Cape Colony for this purpose. The natives and the Boers got into quarrels and local fights, and the Boers tried to get land from them to set up new republics.

MacKenzie was opposed either to Boer or colonial annexation because annexation would not protect the natives. He went to England on furlough in 1882 and campaigned until 1884 for the protectorate system over Bechuanaland after Britain had negotiated treaties with the native chiefs. He wrote articles, interviewed leading statesmen, such as Lord Shaftesbury, lobbied in the House of Commons and spoke all over England. He was able to create a Christian public opinion favorable to control of Bechuanaland by the British government and opposed to the Boers or Rhodes who would not protect the natives. When a Boer delegation from the republics came to England, MacKenzie in an article in the *Contemporary Review* exposed their plan to block the British off from the road to the north. The government in the negotiations refused to let the Boers get control of Bechuanaland.

MacKenzie was appointed as a British resident in Bechuanaland at a salary of £1,200 in 1884. He resigned from the missionary society to take up this government work in which he felt he could better serve the missionary interest for the time being. His task was, as he understood it, to make treaties with the native chiefs and to set up a British protectorate over Bechuanaland. This seems to have been the intention of the British government in the negotiations with the Boers. Cecil Rhodes in Cape Colony opposed MacKenzie because he wanted Cape Colony to annex Bechuanaland directly. In May, 1884, MacKenzie got several chiefs to sign treaties and proclaimed a protectorate before Rhodes succeeded in having him recalled to the coast and in taking over his position as resident. Rhodes did not fare well in his dealings with either the natives or the nearby Boer states.

The British government because of the danger that the Boer republics might annex the area sent an expedition under General Warren to Bechuanaland in 1885. An order-in-council was also promulgated declaring that Bechuanaland was a British protectorate. Thus, in 1885, Bechuanaland finally came under British protection.

Several anti-missionary historians readily admit that the creation of the protectorate was mainly the result of MacKenzie's work in stirring up the Christian public of England

The Scope of Evangelical Reform

to demand protection of the natives from both the Boers and the colonial government, which were equally careless concerning native rights. Without his publicity campaign in England from 1882 to 1884, either the Boers or the colonial government would have annexed this area which is still a protectorate of the British government. MacKenzie's son, in writing his father's biography, depicts the way in which his father was drawn into politics as a means to an end for the sake of his missionary work which would end if the British did not protect the natives. MacKenzie hoped that after a time of training in British law and democracy the natives could have a representative government to govern themselves.

Nyasaland, the areas bordering on Lake Nyasa, was also made a protectorate through missionary influence in order to keep the Portuguese and Arab slave traders from destroying the missionary work of the Scottish Presbyterians in that area. Scottish Christian public opinion was instrumental in forcing the British government to take action.

Livingstone's speech in the Senate House at Cambridge on December 4, 1857, had resulted in the formation of the Anglican Universities Mission by Anglicans. This society sent missionaries in 1861 to the area which he had opened up. In 1875 Scottish Presbyterians also began missionary work on the shores of Lake Nyasa.

Because the missionaries found that trade was taking too much of their time, Christian merchants of Scotland founded the African Lakes Company to take over the task of trade with the natives. It was hoped that legitimate trade could drive out the slave trade. The company had to use force on occasion to stop the Arab slave trade.

Because the Portuguese were still engaged in slave trading and held control of the mouth of the Zambezi up which missonaries and traders had to go to Nyasaland, they threatened to close that river to navigation and placed heavy duties on goods to the missionaries and the company. They sent an expedition into Nyasaland in 1889 under Serpa Pinto for supposedly "scientific" purposes, although it appears the reason was to annex the area. News of this expedition aroused the Scottish at home, and in May of 1889 a delegation of Scottish ministers, peers and members of the House waited upon Prime Minister Salisbury. Scott, the leader, dramatically placed a petition with the names of 11,000 Scottish ministers and elders upon the table with the statement, "This, my Lord, is the voice of Scotland." Salisbury sent an ultimatum to the Portuguese to withdraw their expedition.

Acting Consul Buchanan in Nyasaland declared that it was a British protectorate in 1889. The formal announcement of the protectorate was made by the British government in 1891, and in 1893 it was called the British Central Africa Protectorate. Missionary settlements and the pressure of Scottish Christian opinion forced the annexation of the area as a means of facilitating missionary work among the natives. These men were not imperialists for the sale of imperialism but felt that the natives would be better protected and doors kept open for missions under the British government. Imperialism was to them a legitimate political means to a spiritual end.

Combined missionary and British Christian public opinion at home played an important part in setting up a British protectorate in Uganda. Stanley in several interviews with King Mutesa of Uganda tried to convert the king to Christianity. Stanley then sent a letter of appeal to the *Daily Telegraph* of England which was printed in 1875. As a result of this letter, an anonymous gift of £5,000 was made to the Church Missionary Society if it would send a missionary expedition to Uganda.

Several men were sent out in 1876 and soon found themselves in competition with Roman Catholics and Moslems for the souls of the people of Uganda. When Mutesa died in 1884, his son Mwanga began persecution of the Protestant

The Scope of Evangelical Reform

natives in 1885 and killed 200 of them in the following year. Bishop Tucker came out to lead the work of the society, and after a time Christian work began to prosper.

The Imperial British East Africa Company signed a treaty with Mwanga to help him keep the Germans out of Uganda. Because expenses of the company proved to be so heavy, Lugard, the representative of the company, was ordered to withdraw his forces from Uganda at the end of 1891. Bishop Tucker, who was in England on furlough in 1891, was at a friend's house in Scotland when Sir William Mackinnon docked his yacht for a social call on Tucker's host. Mackinnon, a member of the company, said that Uganda was costing the company £40,000 a year, but that if Tucker could raise £15,000 from friends of the mission he would raise £5,000 from his friends and give £10,000 himself to make up the £30,000 needed to keep the company in Uganda for another year until the British government could see its way clear to step in. Within two weeks the necessary amount was raised, £8,000 of which was subscribed at a missionary meeting in Exeter Hall on the night of October 31, 1891. The company was able to stay in Uganda until the end of 1892.

Meanwhile, Tucker engaged in a campaign to arouse public opinion against the abandonment of Uganda. Gerald Portal, acting as an agent of the British, proclaimed a provisional protectorate over Uganda April 1, 1893. The protectorate was formally announced on June 18, 1894. The timely gift of the Christian supporters of the C.M.S. and the campaign to arouse public opinion kept Uganda under the British crown so that missionary work might go forward. Much of the present economic progress in Uganda must be credited to the efforts of Tucker. He saw in the protectorate a means to a Christian end, the continuance of missionary work in Uganda.

Study of the missionary literature in all of the cases described leaves any unbiased observer with the opinion that the missionaries were not flag-waving imperialists. They supported British control or protectorates as means to an end: the proclamation of the Gospel and the evangelization of the natives under orderly government sympathetic to the interests of the natives.

II. SPIRITUAL AND PHYSICAL FREEDOM FOR THE WORKERS OF ENGLAND

A. Freedom for the Souls and Minds of Working Englishmen

English Evangelicals of the last century were not guilty, as some have suggested, of being alert only to the needs of colored people while they neglected underprivileged Englishmen. Much effort was expended by evangelical Christians, such as Lord Shaftesbury, to create better conditions for the workers of England. They felt that this work was a legitimate expression of their faith. Fame and often fortunes were not considered too great a sacrifice to bring benefit to the poor and oppressed white people in England itself.

Ever since the days of the Reformation, when the reformers emphasized the need of at least an elementary education so people could read the Bible and interpret it for themselves, Protestantism has supported education. Protestants believed that one could find the way to God through the Scriptures if he could read them. The revivalists and the reformers of the eighteenth and nineteenth centuries also emphasized the need for education by the establishment of Sunday schools and weekday schools.

In the late seventeenth century charity schools had been founded by subscriptions in the Anglican Church to educate poor children in reading, writing, arithemtic, moral discipline and the catechism. There were 25,000 children in such schools by 1713. They were the first systematic attempt to give any education to the working class. With this precedent in mind, Wesley and the members of the Holy Club at Oxford founded a school, paid the teacher and even clothed most of the children so they could attend it. Whitefield and Wesley in 1740 started the Kingswood school at Bristol for the children of the miners among whom they began their field preaching. While these were scattered attempts, they testify to the interest of Christians in education at a time when the government as yet had no concern.

A far more important influence in the rise of public elementary education was the Sunday school movement, which must be linked with the warm social zeal of the Evangelicals. Contrary to popular opinion, Robert Raikes was not the founder but the popularizer of the Sunday school movement. Hannah Ball started the first Sunday school in High Wycombe in 1769, at least a decade before Raikes began his school at Gloucester. She informed Wesley in a letter that the children met twice a week on Sunday and Monday and that she thought her work in this fashion would promote "the interest of the church of Christ."

Robert Raikes (1735-1811), however, must have the credit for popularizing the movement. His father was the publisher of the *Gloucester Journal,* and Robert after his father's death took over the paper. He began to visit the prisons of the city and did what he could to help the prisoners. Convinced that work with those who had fallen into crime usually did not succeed, he decided to prevent vice by the education of children. With the help of friends he paid a poor woman to teach the children on Sundays in a school in Sooty Alley. He often had to discipline the pupils before they could be quieted down to learn.

This school, which he began in 1780, he described in the November 3, 1783, issue of his paper. He then opened up several other schools. He received a letter from Hannah More, and his experiment was watched with interest by

John Wesley who had often stayed at the Raikes' home. Raikes also advocated day schools to give free education to the poor and introduced the idea of using older students as teaching monitors to help the teachers. Wilberforce, to whom he was related, was also a visitor at his schools.

This Christian journalist helped to spread the movement all over England. In 1785 a London Society was set up to establish Sunday schools with Henry Thornton as a member of the group, and in ten years it had 65,000 in its schools. Wesley, by word and by writing in his *Arminian Magazine*, encouraged the growth of Sunday schools. J. R. Green, the writer of a popular history of England, credits the Sunday schools with "the beginnings of popular education." Wesley testified in 1784 that he found these schools springing up wherever he went and thought of them as potential "nurseries for Christians." In a letter written in January, 1787, to the founder of such a school in Chester, he wrote that in his opinion they might be "one great means" to "revive religion" in England. When Lord Shaftesbury in 1831 unveiled a statue of Robert Raikes, the claim was made that 1,250,000 were in Sunday schools.

The poetess Hannah More (1745-1833), a close friend of Horace Walpole, Joshua Reynolds, the actor Garrick and the great Samuel Johnson, was converted partly through the influence of John Newton. She became a friend of Wilberforce, and when he visited her and her sisters in 1789, they went to Cheddar not too far from the sisters' home. They were so shocked by the ignorance and distress there that they set up Sunday schools and paid a teacher £30 a year. The work grew until they soon had 500 in their schools, in which the Bible and the catechism were taught. In ten years this grew into a complex of schools caring for 3,000 in twelve parishes. For several years Thornton gave the sisters £600 and Wilberforce £400 annually for their work.

The Scope of Evangelical Reform 105

Lord Shaftesbury became interested in the Ragged School movement which was begun in 1798 by a tailor, Thomas Cranfield, to care for children who were even too ragged to attend Sunday school. Many of the teachers donated their services and, in 1844, forty of them banded together in a Ragged School Union and persuaded Shaftesbury to become their first president. It will be noticed that the Factory Act of 1833, which was largely the result of his work, called for two hours of school a day for children working in factories. In 1839 he persuaded the government to raise the educational grant from £30,000 a year to £813,400 a year. He was desirous of having moral and spiritual education based on the Bible in any public school system. Between 1844 and 1870 nearly 300,000 children had received some education in the Ragged Schools. Thus the products of the eighteenth century revivals were an important force in the rise of popular, free, compulsory education in England.

That Evangelicals did not entirely neglect higher education is demonstrated by the activities of Whitefield. When Samuel Davies and Gilbert Tennent went to England in 1753 to get financial help for the little log college that became Princeton University, they looked to Whitefield for help. When the library at Harvard was destroyed in 1764, Whitefield wrote to England to get books for a new library. In 1740 a building was erected in Philadelphia by his supporters as a charity school for the free education of poor children. This became an academy, then Philadelphia College, and ultimately the University of Pennsylvania. A statue erected in 1914 declared him to be "the inspirer and original trustee" of the Charity School which was the forerunner of the University. It was also said that he solicited the first donations for the library of the University. On the pedestal he is proclaimed as the "zealous advocate and patron of higher education" in the colonies.

B. Physical Freedom for Englishmen

The needs of the total human personality interested these godly men. They wanted to provide for the physical as well as the mental well-being of men, knowing that the two aspects of humanity were closely related. Extensive and arduous labor, costly in energy and fortune, went into freeing Englishmen from many kinds of physical bondage so that they could be free sons of God as well as free Englishmen.

1. Prison Reform

The relief of prisoners in the jails of England was a matter of interest to Wesley from his university days. He and other members of the Holy Club visited debtors in the debtor prison and felons in the jail at Oxford. From then on he visited and urged upon his followers the duty of visitation of prisons, publicized bad prison conditions, and ardently supported movements to reform the prisons. This interest even extended to the enemies of England. When he saw the need of 1,100 French prisoners of war in a prison near Bristol in 1759, he took up an offering of £24 in an evening meeting at Bristol. With the money he provided articles of clothing and persuaded the city authorities to provide blankets. Despite personal anguish and often in the face of physical danger his followers carried out his advice in accord with the teachings of Christ to visit those in prisons. The Conference of 1778 made the visit of prisons a duty of Methodist ministers.

The Methodists did not go beyond visitation and the publicizing of evils in the prisons though they did support the work of prison reformers. The work of prison reform was begun by John Howard, Elizabeth Fry and her brother-in-law, T. Fowell Buxton. John Howard (1726-1790) freely acknowledged the inspiration of Wesley's example in his work for the reform of prisons. Wesley, in his *Journal*, characterized Howard as one of Europe's "greatest men" and, according to Howard, encouraged him to go on with his work.

Howard was a sickly child whose parents died when he was in his teens. His father had done well in the upholstery and carpet business so young Howard was able to tour the Continent. On his way to Portugal in 1756, he was taken prisoner by a French privateer and thrown into a prison in France where, until he was able to secure the release of himself and his fellows, he experienced the rigors of prison life.

In 1773 he was appointed High Sheriff of Bedfordshire. He was shocked at the number of people imprisoned without trial and at the practice of the jailers securing their fees from the prisoners, who either had to starve or be cared for by their own families if they could not pay the fees. He asked the county quarter-session whether the jailer could be given a salary. Howard was told that such an arrangement could be made if he were able to find other countries following that practice. This tour of investigation started him on his career as a prison reformer.

In 1774 he gave evidence before a committee of the House of Commons investigating prisons. Laws were passed in that session ending the practice of jailers' collecting fees from their prisoners and improving sanitary conditions in prisons. He visited prisons in the British Isles, France, Germany and Holland in 1775 and 1776 and wrote a book on the state of prisons in England and Wales. During the remainder of his life his travels took him all over Europe until his death by fever in Russia. In the course of his travels he spent £30,000 of his own money and traveled 50,000 miles in his endeavor to bring about prison reform in England and the countries of Europe. This godly Evangelical, who belonged to a Congregational church, while doing this work carried the burden of care of an insane son.

Elizabeth Fry (1780-1845), whose sister married Buxton, was first interested in prison work by Stephen Grellet, a French nobleman who became a Quaker. From 1811, she made almost daily visits to women in Newgate prison and visited almost every transport that left England with prisoners for the penal colonies between 1818 and 1841. She gave clothes, started schools and read the Bible to the women prisoners in Newgate. Her work at Newgate and in the transports constituted her main contribution to the needs of the prisoners, but the influence of her life and preaching should not be discounted. Any reading of the sources of information concerning Buxton gives a clear impression of her influence upon his decision to dedicate the early part of his career in the House of Commons to the cause of prison reform. Wilberforce, who knew her, always found time to support any measure to better conditions in prisons, and he supported Romilly and Mackintosh in their attempts to cut down the large number of trivial crimes for which the punishment might be execution. Christ's command to visit those in prisons certainly was not neglected by the Evangelicals who were products of the great revivals in England.

2. *Emancipation of the Insane*

If Wilberforce was the chief champion of the colored slaves, Shaftesbury must be considered the champion of the mentally ill and oppressed laboring classes of England. Shaftesbury's first speech in Parliament and the earliest legistlation for which he was responsible were designed to improve conditions in the mental institutions of England. To him no social evil was beyond remedy if the conscience of Christians could be aroused to action by factual information. His work can never be understood apart from his love of the Scriptures and his faith in Christ as his Saviour.

Anthony Ashley Cooper, the seventh Earl of Shaftesbury (1801-1885) was the son of a politician, who was a poor landlord to his tenants, and of a mother whose only interest was society. The father's harsh cold manner and the belief of both parents that children should be neither heard nor seen

The Scope of Evangelical Reform

threw the child upon his own resources from an early age. Fortunately for him, he had a godly friend, Maria Millis, the housekeeper who was a devout Christian. She lavished her love on the child and at her knee he learned to pray and listened to the reading of the Scriptures. The deep impression of her life upon him was revealed in his often showing his friends the gold watch she had willed to him—he would wear no other—and stating that she was the best friend he had ever had in the world.

He kept up daily prayer and Bible study when he went away to school at the age of seven. Manor House, where he was first sent to school, was distasteful to him because of filth, bullying and neglect. He feared vacations because they would bring him into contact with his parents.

At twelve he was sent to Harrow which he liked much better. It was while here that the event occurred which caused him to dedicate himself to the cause of the poor and oppressed of England. He heard and soon saw a shouting, cursing, drunken band of fellows carrying a coffin to the cemetery. They let the coffin fall because of their drunken unsteadiness. Shaftesbury was amazed that the body of a poor and friendless man should be so treated and then and there on Harrow Hill dedicated himself to God to aid the poor and friendless.

He learned little at Harrow and spent the years after leaving there in Derbyshire with a clergyman who had married his cousin. Here he spent most of his time with his horse and dogs. He was sent to Christ Church College at Oxford and obtained his A.B. with first class honors in classics in 1822, his M.A. in 1832, and an advanced honorary degree in 1841. He spent the years between 1822 and 1826 in reading and travel on the Continent.

He wrote in his diary on December 13, 1825, that he had a "great mind to found a policy upon the Bible" in order to observe "the strictest justice, and not only cold justice, but active benevolence" in public life. He entered the House of Commons after his election in 1826. Though he joined the Conservative or Tory party, he always put principle above party. On April 22, 1827, he wrote in his diary, "I desire to be useful in my generation," and on December 17 prayed that if wealth ever came to him that he would have "a heart and spirit to lay it out for man's happiness and God's glory." He desired "the advancement of religion and the increase of human happiness" in order to be useful to his God and to his country.

His first speech in the House in 1828 was on behalf of lunatics. Bedlam, whose name is now a word signifying confusion, was an asylum near London. People for a small fee were admitted by the attendants to get amusement from watching lunatics chained to walls with only filthy straw for a bed, from seeing them goaded by the keepers or spun in rotary chairs or dropped into surprise baths to subdue them.

An act of Parliament in 1774 had given local magistrates the power to lock up the insane, and to regulate private asylums. This act bettered conditions little because physicians examining the houses could only report abuses which were not corrected. In June, 1827, Robert Gordon formed a committee which reported on the condition of the insane asylums, and he moved, in 1828, a bill seconded by Shaftesbury, which became law. It took the power of supervising asylums from the College of Physicians and gave it to a commission of which Shaftesbury was a member and after 1829 the chairman. This act and two others in 1845, for which Shaftesbury was responsible, made it impossible to commit sane people to asylums to get rid of them and to abuse those who were in asylums. The asylums became hospitals instead of prisons. These acts were the Magna Charta of the insane, and the young member of the House had indeed worthily upheld the honor of God and promoted the happiness of his fellows.

The Scope of Evangelical Reform

3. Emancipation of the Workers of England

If Wilberforce was the great emancipator of colored slaves, Shaftesbury was the emancipator of the industrial wage-slaves which the workers of England had become in the early days of the Industrial Revolution. In both cases the inspiration for their work was their faith, and apart from their personal faith in Christ as Saviour and a love for men as potential or actual sons of God one cannot explain their work. Shaftesbury took up political life as a career because it seemed to him the best way by which he could be useful to his generation. Because his party was not in office during the interim between his work for the insane and that for the workers, he studied for his master's degree at Oxford. In 1830 he married Lady Emily Cowper, who encouraged him greatly in his work. When he was re-elected for the County of Dorset in 1831, he incurred nearly £6,000 of election expenses which he had to pay himself. He soon became known with good reason as the "working man's friend."

Robert Peel earlier had Parliament pass acts which applied to children working in the cotton factories. The act of 1802 had limited the work of pauper children, whom the authorities often farmed out to factory owners, to twelve hours a day and provided that they should have decent quarters and religious education. Another bill in 1819 was broadened to include all children and provided that no child under nine could work in a factory and those from nine to sixteen could work only twelve hours a day apart from meals. These acts, however, only applied to cotton mills and provided no means of inspection. It is little wonder that the mill owners paid scant attention to them.

Other evangelical Tories had begun the work which Shaftesbury later took up. The expert propagandist of the movement was Richard Oastler (1789-1861) who was to the movement on behalf of the workers what Macaulay and earlier Clarkson had been to the abolitionists. Oastler, who never left the Anglican church but was disinherited by his father when he became a Methodist, served as a steward on an estate.

A visit with John Wood, a godly manufacturer of Bradford, led to Oastler's decision to devote himself to the cause of factory workers. On September 29, 1830, his friend Wood described the evils of the factory system to him, and after Oastler went to bed his host called him into his bedroom and told him he could not sleep for thinking of the evils of the system. He asked Oastler to promise to do his best to bring about the end of the evils of the factory system which were contrary to the Bible which he had been reading. Oastler, who stated that he felt they were in the presence of God, solemnly promised to do his best and claimed that by the grace of God he would be faithful to that charge and his promise. He also had the support of John Fielden who owned one of the largest factories in the world at that time. Immediately after that Oastler wrote a letter called "Yorkshire Slavery" to the Leeds *Mercury*. The letter described conditions of labor in the factories of that country. Until he was imprisoned for several years for a debt of £2,000 to the man whom he served as steward, this six-foot, stentorian-voiced man worked untiringly to support first Sadler and then Shaftesbury in their attempts to secure legislation to better factory conditions. Released when friends raised money to pay his debt, the "Factory King" continued to serve the cause by agitating for a ten-hour day by letters to the press, public speeches and petitions.

Michael Sadler (1780-1835), an evangelical Anglican of Huguenot descent, who even served as superintendent of a Methodist Sunday school, was the leader of the factory reform movement until he was succeeded by Shaftesbury in 1833. This Tory importer of Irish linen did not care too much for business and as he began to read economics he became conscious of the plight of the worker. As early as 1823, an Anglican minister, G. S. Bull, found him worried about factory children. Sadler opposed the *laissez-faire* economic theories which taught there were fixed economic laws governing society, rendering parliamentary action on behalf of the workers useless.

He became Wilberforce's political agent and friend and, in 1829, entered the House of Commons as a member from Newcastle. With Oastler supporting him by propaganda and mass meetings of up to 16,000 persons in the country, Sadler tried in December, 1831, to get a factory act to secure a ten-hour day for children in the textile mills. Instead, the House set up a committee in 1832 to examine evidence.

This committee, with Sadler as its chairman, began to hear evidence in April, 1832, and examined eighty-nine witnesses, half of whom were workers. The report, which was made in August, 1832, was supplemented by private reports by Fielden and Wood. These reports told of thirteen- to sixteen-hour days for children and in rush seasons even up to twenty-four hours of consecutive work except for thirty minutes to eat. Some mills ran twenty-four hours with two shifts of children working twelve hours each shift. When one shift got out of bed, those on the other shift would take over the beds. Children who did not keep up because of exhaustion would be brutally strapped by the supervisor. The moist hot air of the factory and leaning over the machines stunted the growth of many and caused illnesses. No guards on machinery made accidents inevitable. The reformers demonstrated that children would walk seventeen to thirty miles a day in tending the machines. Unfortunately Sadler's seat was eliminated by the redistribution under the Reform Bill of 1832, and he was defeated when he ran for election in Leeds. His health never recovered from the strain of the task of drawing up the report of the committee on factory conditions in 1832.

Someone had to be found to assume parliamentary leadership of the factory reform movement. Southey, in a letter to Shaftesbury on January 13, 1833, spoke of the loss the movement had suffered and plaintively asked who would deal with the issue "of our white slave trade." G. S. Bull, at the suggestion of Sir Andrew Agnew, a Scottish member of the House, asked Shaftesbury to take Sadler's place. After consultation with friends and prayer, he asked the opinion of his wife who told him that it was his duty and the consequences could be left to God. She urged him to "Go forward, and to victory."

He looked upon his work as a duty to God and the poor. Shaftesbury's faith in God expressed in loving action on behalf of the workers had behind it his sense of stewardship in the light of the Second Coming of Christ. He was of the opinion that what was morally right must be politically right and what was morally wrong could never be politically right. He would use the law to restrain those who were vicious and to protect the oppressed. During his career in the House until 1851 and in Lords from 1851 to 1885, he remained true to such principles in his fight for the poor and oppressed of England. During fifty-seven of sixty years of public service he received no money for his work, though others on the same commissions were receiving public salaries. He also turned down high positions which were offered to him. It is little wonder that he won the hearts of the workers of England. They looked to him as their champion after he took over parliametnary leadership of the struggle in 1833.

He introduced a bill in February, 1833, in the House to stop children under nine from working, to limit hours for those under eighteen to ten hours a day and eight on Saturday with complete exclusion of any night work. The manufacturing interests won delay by asking for a Royal Commission of Inquiry although all the evidence necessary to show the evils of the system had been amassed by Sadler's Report. Shaftesbury was always careful to be sure of his facts and made it a rule to see everything himself. This meant careful examination of factories, machinery, homes and the pitiful condition of the workers. He could always speak from experience on behalf of his beloved workers. The government agreed to introduce a bill in order to avoid the even more strict bill Shaftesbury would have introduced. No child was to work in the textile factories until the age of ten. According to the government bill, those under thirteen were limited to nine hours a day in a forty-eight-hour week; those under eighteen to twelve hours a day and sixty-nine hours a week. Two hours of schooling each day were mandatory. In order to enforce this act inspectors were provided. The act became law in the summer of 1833. Even though it was a government bill, it would not have been passed unless the Evangelicals had pushed for it with the aid of the radicals. Thus, in 1833, both colored slaves and white workers were granted freedom.

The 1833 bill did not work too well until after 1836. Of the 1,948 violations reported by the inspectors in 1835, only in 177 cases were there convictions by courts.

Shaftesbury and his friends wanted a ten-hour day for workers. He continued to agitate for it even though the workers for a short time turned against him because they thought that he had betrayed them by accepting the government bill instead of insisting upon his own stricter bill. In 1840 Shaftesbury became the chairman of a Select Committee to study the operation of the act of 1833. He wanted a ten-hour bill, but got nowhere because Peel in 1842 expressed his opposition to such a limitation of working hours. The government bill, which became law in 1844, limited work for children from their thirteenth until eighteenth birthdays to twelve hours a day. This fell short of the ten-hour day the reformers desired. In 1847 Fielden, after some years of agitation, introduced a bill limiting the hours of work for women and children in textile factories to ten hours per day. This bill passed. The ten-hour day and a fifty-eight-hour week became a reality for many of the workers of England in 1848, when the final provisions of the bill were put into effect. Although Shaftesbury had little to do with the passage of the bill of 1847, much of the credit should go to him for laying the groundwork by producing irrefutable evidence. In fact, none of the great factory acts were personally drawn up by him, but he was really the "moving spirit behind them all."

In 1840 he had asked for a committee to study the matter of women and children working in mines and by 1842 the report was complete. It revealed horrible tales of some children working in mines at the age of four and five and most not over eight. Some had the task of staying twelve to fourteen hours a day in cold damp niches without light so that they could open and shut doors to permit loads of coal to pass and to maintain proper ventilation. Other children had to help push coal carts with their heads. The committee found several who had bald spots because of this. Women were pulling carts carrying over 200 pounds of coal by means of a strap fastened around their waists. Often low shafts made it necessary for them to crawl on their hands and knees. One child of nine in charge of an engine which operated a mine elevator left his work to chase a mouse and three miners were killed. Girls of fifteen to eighteen years worked along with women in the mines. Moral conditions in many instances were found to be very low.

The Report so shocked the House of Commons in 1842 that when Shaftesbury presented a bill to take girls, women and boys under thirteen out of mines and to permit no very young person to work in a place where the lives of others were involved, his moving speech brought about its rapid passage. In the final bill the age of boys in mines was lowered to ten years and the age of engineers from twenty-one to fifteen. The bill also provided for inspectors. Again the miners were indebted to Shaftesbury as their successful champion. In his work on their behalf he visited and inspected mines personally in order to have first-hand evidence.

He also became interested in the fate of chimney sweeps who were sent up chimneys to sweep the flues of soot. In order to harden their skin, the masters would often soak them in brine, then dry them and soak them again. If they were afraid to climb chimneys, as many of them were because they were so young, the master would often light a damp fire of straw under them so they would be forced to continue up the flue and finish their work. Some of these children, mostly orphans, were from four to eight years of age. Shaftesbury persuaded Parliament to pass an act in 1864 which prohibited children under sixteen from becoming chimney sweeps. In 1875 he obtained a bill which banned the use of sweeps and forced the substitution of machinery for this task.

He also took up the cudgel on behalf of workers in the brickyards of England. He found 30,000 in the brickyards who were from three-and-a-half to seventeen years of age and whose health suffered because they had to work alternately with cold clay and the hot kilns. Legislation was passed to protect them.

He became interested in conditions in lodging houses for workers, and visited and inspected many so carefully that on occasion he found that he was bringing home lice and bed bugs on his person. In 1851 he secured legislation for the inspeciton and registration of lodging houses.

As a landowner he was not blind to the needs of the people on his lands. One should remember that he planted orchards, built new cottages and schools and rejuvenated the parish church on his estate. He also banned the truck system which forced the people to deal only with stores on the estate. This work resulted in a model village.

He became interested in the needs of soldiers during the Crimean War after Florence Nightingale, the founder of a real nursing profession in England, got him to read government reports telling of the privations and sufferings of soldiers through neglect and incompetence. At the suggestion of Shaftesbury a Sanitary Commission was sent out in 1855 by the War Department to study conditions in hospitals in the Crimea. He drew up the instructions to the Commissioners and with the help of Miss Nightingale organized its membership. This Commission, according to Florence Nightingale, "saved the British Army."

While a member of the Lunacy Commission Shaftesbury refused to take any salary although other members were paid £1,500 a year. Even after he inherited his father's estate, he was poor and had to sacrifice to educate his eight children, and in order to improve conditions for the tenants on the estate he had to sell family pictures from the family gallery. He declined high office many times and refused the honor of the Order of the Garter and burial in Westminster Abbey. A grateful England did, however, give him an Abbey funeral service before his burial on the family estate in 1885. His life exemplified the family motto which was "Love, Serve."

Rich and poor alike testified to his generous aid to any in need or oppressed by society. Although a protectionist land-owning Tory, the need of the Irish in the difficult days of the potato crop failure of 1845 and 1846 caused him to vote for the repeal of duties on grain in order that bread might become cheaper. This would automatically cut the income of his own class because it lowered the price paid for grain. He was opposed to extending the vote to the middle or lower class because he thought that democracy was based on the, to him false, assumption of the perfectibility of man. Even this seeming inconsistency was based upon his opposition to rationalism.

This account of the work of Evangelicals, whether they were Dissenters or Anglican, has demonstrated the combination of a desire to meet the needs of men's bodies as well as to convert their souls. These men who had been converted themselves and who accepted the Bible as the Word of God, believed that religion should have a social expression and that faith should become evident in loving service in the social order. They agreed with Paul that men were "created in Christ Jesus unto good works" (Eph. 2:10). This commission they carried out at the expense in many cases of fortune, fame and even health in order that they might glorify God by seeking the welfare of His potential or actual sons.

Chapter IV

THE SPIRIT OF EVANGELICAL REFORM

IN THE ACCOUNT of the broad scope of social activities of the Evangelicals, the subject of the previous chapter, the motivation for such consecration and self-sacrifice was not developed. What motives would cause a man, such as Zachary Macaulay, to devote his time to the cause of the abolition of slavery to the point that his fortunes, entrusted to others, were endangered and even lost? What would cause Shaftesbury to serve for fifty-seven out of sixty years in public service without any remuneration and lead him to sell valued family portraits to raise money to improve the homes on the estates which he had inherited from his father? Similar questions might be asked concerning any of those who have been considered. Did their humanitarianism have, as so much of reform in England in this period had, mere rational motives? Any fair examination of their writings will reveal that the motivation proceeded primarily from the Bible. The Bible led them by faith to Christ, and Christ inspired in them a love that issued in dedicated service to their fellows.

I. THE BASIS OF WESLEY'S SOCIAL THOUGHT

Some consideration should be given to the thinking of John Wesley on this question. Wesley did not himself give quite so much attention to activities on the social level as

Whitefield did. Whitefield linked a passion for souls with a zeal for social service that resulted in the founding of Bethesda Orphange near Savannah, Georgia. But Wesley was an innovator in such activities as the first free medical dispensary in England, and his Methodist followers loyally supported by vote and petition the work of reformers, such as Shaftesbury and Wilberforce. It will be remembered that Wesley wrote letters of encouragement to Granville Sharp in his fight to abolish slavery by judicial decision in England and wrote his last letter to Wilberforce to encourage him to be an "Athanasius" against the world in his fight against the slave trade.

Wesley earnestly sought to be pleasing to God from the earliest years of his life. He had been one of the most zealous members of the Holy Club at Oxford. He had faithfully read the Greek New Testament and had taken the communion according to the Church of England rites regularly. He had sought to please God also by works of charity. He was the leader in prison visitation and the provision of educational facilities for the children of the poor around Oxford. When the opportunity came to go to Georgia, he wrote, on October 10,1735, to his friend Dr. John Burton, a Trustee of the Colony of Georgia, that his main reason for going to Georgia was the hope that he might save his own soul. While he was in America, August Spangenberg, a Moravian leader, asked him if he knew Christ. When Wesley replied that he knew Jesus Christ was the Saviour of the world, Spangenberg pressed the question whether Wesley knew that He was his Saviour. Wesley replied that he did, but in his later writings he admitted that he was aware that he really did not know Christ in a personal way.

The bravery and calm faith of Moravians during a bad storm while en route to Georgia impressed Wesley. When he returned to England in 1738, Peter Böhler, another Moravian, was a spiritual counselor to him. Finally, on May

24, 1738, in a little meeting in Aldersgate Street, London, as Wesley was listening to the reading of Luther's *Preface to the Epistle to the Romans,* he became aware that his heart was "strangely warmed" and he trusted in "Christ alone for salvation." An assurance of the forgiveness of his sins came over him. This experience was for Wesley the parallel to Paul's experience on the road to Damascus. It became a starting point in his life. The doctrine of justification by faith became not only one of the cardinal doctrines of his system but also the foundation of his preaching in church, chapel or the open air. It was also the basic force which led him to work of a social nature. This inward personal experience of salvation involved the awareness of sin, the need of repentance, faith in Christ and a resulting assurance of forgiveness of sins. This was the aim of his evangelism; he believed that it was his "bounden duty" to preach "plain, old Bible Christianity" to all who would listen.

Wesley also believed that one who was justified and made free from sin by faith in Christ had his heart suffused with a love to God. This love to God should be manifested in a love for his fellow men that would result in social activity for their good. For him there could be no separation between love for God and love for man. This love for man could be best expressed in any social activity that would bring good to man and glory to God.

In a sermon on Matthew 5:13-16, Wesley expressed himself strongly with the assertion that Christianity was "essentially a social religion" and one would destroy it if one kept it to oneself. As far as he was concerned society could never be reconstructed by any theory which ignored the redemption of the individual. The thrust of his gospel was from an inward, personal, individual experience of salvation to the outward or external social expression of that experience in service. Love to God would beget love to man in service. In the preface to the first Methodist hymnal, he wrote, in 1739, only about a year after his conversion, that Christianity knew "no religion but social, no holiness but social holiness." Wesley believed there could be no real profession without practice, no faith that did not manifest itself with the force of love. The essence of social reformation was the regeneration of the soul. Paul's classic union of faith toward God and love toward the saints (Eph. 1:15) was certainly understood and practiced by Wesley and his followers.

Because he was so conscious of what Christ had done for him, he was keenly aware of the value of a soul. It was this consciousness that made him and Whitefield such passionate evangelists. But their love for their fellows growing out of a love of God to them in salvation gave them a sense of stewardship of time, talents, and property for the glory of God and the good of others.

Only as one was free spiritually could one be a true Christian steward. A steward would follow Wesley's third rule of stewardship, "give all you can," as faithfully as the first two rules, which urged him to "gain all you can" and "save all you can." One would meet the needs of his family, then those of the circle of believers, and would finally express love to all in the faithful stewardship of the possessions which God had been pleased to give him. It is little wonder that Wesley liked Christ's words in Matthew 25:34-36 concerning the feeding of the hungry and visiting those who were sick and in prison. The Methodists fed the poor, visited and ministered to the needs of the sick and visited prisons to help even those who were prisoners of war. Wesley had little use for the saint who was not expressing his love to God in loving service to others in need within his own social order.

II. THE SPIRIT OF WILBERFORCE'S SOCIAL ACTIVITY

Although Wesley was a clergyman of the Church of England and Wilberforce was a layman, their views as to the origin of the impulse to engage in social service and the motive for participation therein were similar. Wilberforce became conscious of his sinfulness and his lost condition during a journey on the Continent with Isaac Milner in 1784 when they read together Philip Doddridge's *Rise and Progress of Religion*. On their next trip, in the fall of 1785, they read together the Greek New Testament to see whether the things about which Doddridge spoke were in the Bible.

Wilberforce was under deep conviction during that winter and thought of pride as his greatest stumbling block. He talked to John Newton without receiving much help, but a visit to Newton's church to hear him preach brought Wilberforce to the acceptance of Christ as his Saviour by faith alone sometime late in December, 1785. He was conscious of the vicarious death of Christ on the cross as the only ground for pardon. His sons record that later, when he heard of the death of a friend, he said that forgiveness would come if one fled to God "pleading the blood of Jesus." This was in contrast to the prevailing view of his class. To them religion was primarily an ethical matter, and salvation merely involved attendance at the services of the church and other religious activities. This view clashed with Wilberforce's new conviction that "the renovation of our corrupted nature" and "the attainment of every Christian grace" could come alone through faith in the work of Christ for us.

Having been converted, Wilberforce sought the will of God for his life. In 1787 he became interested in the reformation of manners and morals in England as his God-given task. In that year he wrote in his journal that God had set before him two objects, "the suppression of the slave trade and the reformation of manners." He believed that he was providentially led to the cause of abolition. This sense of dedication to a divine commission never left him during the long course of his struggle with the slave trade. He wrote to Babington in 1821 that being the instrument of abolition of the slave trade and the opening of India to the gospel were the greatest blessings of his life.

There is also some evidence that he did his work with the consciousness of the Second Coming of Christ. On January 20, 1792, he wrote to William Manning that one should try constantly to have the "frame of mind" and the "course of conduct" with which one could be said "to be waiting for the appearance of Jesus Christ." Love to God should be manifested in loving service to man with a view to occupying the time properly until death or the Second Coming of Christ.

Nowhere are Wilberforce's views more clearly set forth than in his book which appeared in 1797. The full title, *A Practical View of the Prevailing Religious System of Professed Christians in the Higher and Middle Classes in this Country Contrasted with Real Christianity*, is descriptive of the thesis which Wilberforce set forth. The idea for the book first came to him on a visit to Bath with Henry Venn in 1793. The first draft was completed in 1797 and the book was published on April 2 by a none-too-enthusiastic Mr. Caddell, who only agreed to print it if Wilberforce's name were on the book as author. The 500 copies were sold in a few days, and by August the book was in the fifth edition and 7,500 copies had been sold. Fifteen impressions of two editions were sold in England by 1826 and twenty-five impressions were necessary to satisfy the demands of the American market to that date. Society took up the book and it became a "sensation" at the fashionable resort of Bath. Wilberforce sent a copy to Pitt asking him to read especially the sixth chapter, which dealt with the need of politics being based upon religion. Burke received comfort from it in his dying hours. The book was also translated into French, German, Italian, Spanish and Dutch. In some respects this book became the manifesto of the evangelical party and of the Clapham Sect.

Wilberforce's contrast between Christianity and the religion of the upper classes of his day pointed out the failure of the latter to recognize the primacy of Christianity in the life, the temporal nature of the present, the coming judgment at death, the refusal to face the doctrine and the results of original sin and the folly of attempting good works without faith. An "amiable temper and useful lives" were insufficient to save. Because of the "scanty and erroneous system" of the religion of his day, because religion is everyone's business and because its advancement is tied in intimately with the temporal interests of society, even though he was "a political man" rather than a theologian or preacher, Wilberforce set forth his ideas of true religion.

After emphasizing the need of "diligent perusal of the Holy Scriptures," Wilberforce wrote that man is "tainted with sin" in his nature "radically and to the very core." This affects all the descendants of Adam. He wanted people to remember that they were "fallen creatures, born in sin and naturally depraved." In addition to this internal defect, there was the external solicitation to sin by the activity of Satan.

Once one had accepted the doctrine of man's sinfulness and consequent need of salvation by a supernatural power, the way of salvation by faith in the work of Christ on the cross became a possibility. That and not the average morality of the day, which was not above that of a "good Deist, Mussulman or Hindu," was the way of salvation. Ethics would not produce salvation, but salvation would result in an ethical life. Salvation would involve the "enthusiasm" which many in that day condemned in Methodists. Faith in Christ was the foundation for the "practical" Christianity which he was advocating. Amiability, so acceptable in society (and Wilberforce had an unusual share of it), was not enough.

Chapter six of his work was devoted to a consideration of the relationship of Christianity to the social order, especially in the realm of politics. Wilberforce was convinced that religion generally promoted "the temporal welfare of political

The Spirit of Evangelical Reform 127

communities," but Christianity particularly did so if morals were not divorced from doctrine. "True Christian benevolence" would always be occupied with the production of "happiness to the utmost of its power." True religion is adapted to the "preservation and healthfulness of political communities." Thus a Christian nation would be blessed in both its domestic and foreign policies. Wilberforce was convinced that economic or political problems were basically moral problems to which the dynamic and ethic of Christianity must be applied. Christianity would oppose selfishness, "the moral distemper of political communities." "True religion" and "pure morality" would in any case be conducive to the "well-being of states, and the preservation of civil order." Wilberforce believed that national problems in England were due "to the decline of religion and morality." In his journal in 1793, Wilberforce wrote of his intention to set aside in that week a day for fasting and religious exercises to seek God and to pray for "political direction" for God's blessing on his parliamentary labors and on his country.

Wilberforce's labors on behalf of the Negro slaves had their origin in his experience of conversion, which drew out his heart in love to God, and had their motivation in the consequent love for man. The Scriptures, which commanded such love to God and man, he accepted as the criterion for his opinions and actions. Negroes were fellow-creatures who should be helped rather than exploited by their white brethren because Christianity has an equal regard for all human beings.

Never did Wilberforce let social service become an end of religion; rather it was a product. In writing to a friend he stated that the salvation of one was of much more value than "the mere temporal happiness" even of millions. In addition, Christians must constantly attempt to have a mental attitude and a pattern of conduct with which they could "be justly said to be waiting for the appearance of the Lord

Jesus Christ." These were the principles which were set forth in his famous three and a half-hour speech when he introduced his motion for the abolition of the slave trade in 1789 and in the pamphlets which he wrote against the trade. One cannot read *A Practical View*, his speeches, journal or letters without becoming aware of these principles which were an outgrowth of the dynamic which became his by faith in Christ as his Saviour.

III. THE SPIRIT OF SHAFTESBURY'S SERVICE TO THE WORKERS OF ENGLAND

Shaftesbury's services to the working people of England were inspired by motives similar to those which we have seen in the life of Wilberforce with one exception: Shaftesbury had a deeper conviction of the imminent possibility of Christ's return to earth. His every energy was given to the promotion of such measures as expediting the return of the Jews to their own land so that the prophecies which he believed spoke of that return and Jewish possession of the land before the coming of Christ might be fulfilled. Thus the last barrier to Christ's return might be removed.

Shaftesbury took his stand with the Evangelicals within the Church of England. He was, as he put it "an Evangelical of the Evangelicals" by conviction, and he ascribed most of the "great philanthropic reforms" of the nineteenth century to this party. Any objective view of social history in England in the first half of the nineteenth century will substantiate this viewpoint. When Hodder, his biographer, began the task of writing his biography, Shaftesbury reminded him that he was an Evangelical and that no biography would properly represent him that did not give large place to his religious views.

The reformer took his stand within the Reformation tradition with his assertions concerning the right of private interpretation of the Scripture by the individual and the decla-

The Spirit of Evangelical Reform 129

ration of the inspiration of that Scripture. The Bible was to be the infallible rule of faith and life for the individual and apart from it there could be no knowledge of salvation. He took the position that he would never in action or belief go where he could not have the authority and guidance of the Scriptures behind him. Bible study and prayer were important parts of his life. Constantly in his diary occur references to times of fellowship with God in prayer and enlightenment from the study of the Bible. When the great debate concerning the setting up of the public schools took place about 1870, Shaftesbury demanded that the teaching of the Bible be not an extra but an essential in the school hours in order to give the children an adequate ethical and religious foundation for life. He stood for "the Word of God as the basis of education" in every situation.

For that reason he was a staunch opponent of liberal criticism of the Scriptures. When Bishop Colenso in 1866 expressed doubt concerning the Mosaic authorship of the Pentateuch, Shaftesbury strongly opposed him. For him rationalism was a greater danger to true religion than was "Romanism" which he also steadfastly opposed because it set up a different authority for life, the church, instead of the Bible. He told members of the British and Foreign Bible Society at their annual meeting in 1851 that "the Bible and the Bible alone" was the religion of Protestants and that this truth had been established at the Reformation. Any concession on the point of the authority of Scripture would be dangerous, he believed, and would open the door to all kinds of errors.

Because Shaftesbury believed the Bible to be the Word of God, he was convinced of the truth of the total depravity of man which he found in experience as well as in the Bible. It was this depravity which left man helpless to do the will of God without an experience of justification by faith based upon the atonement of Christ upon the cross of Calvary. For him the "fundamental turning point" of religion, without which it would have no content, was through the shed blood of Christ. Justification by faith in the work of Christ on the cross was for Shaftesbury "the grand doctrine" which was the "Keystone of the Reformation." Faith in Christ's work alone could bring forgiveness and bring the enlightenment of the understanding by which the character would be transformed. Then one could safely entrust the events of life to the hands of God. Maria Millis, his friend during his early childhood, had indeed taught him well, and the lessons he learned from the Bible which she had read to him became the guiding principle of his life. His experience of justification by faith dated from the time in his early childhood when he had been under her tutelage.

Shaftesbury, like Wesley, had had no use for a faith that would not manifest itself in loving service for the glory of God and the good of man. It was no accident that the words, "Love, Serve" were chosen as the motto of his family and that, when the workers of England erected a memorial to him in Piccadilly Circus, Shaftesbury was depicted as the Christian Eros who put Christian love into political life. In his diary entry for Sunday, January 9, 1852, he pointed out that the mass of people have no charity and added his wish that the translators of the Bible had retained the word love instead of substituting the word charity for love. Only love, he thought, would contribute to the "temporal and eternal welfare of mankind." Love to Christ and His creatures alone would constitute the "absolutely essential and practical" application of Christianity. He stated his belief in the diary entry for December 20, 1860, that God had called him "to the relief of the factory population" and that He had granted him the strength to do that work adequately. It was "a love for the whole infantive world" that led to his strenuous labors on behalf of the children working in the factories of England, cleaning its chimneys, making its bricks or mining its coal. This love led him to have the honor of God as his first principle and the welfare of men as his second principle of public service. Unless the administration of the country was founded on truth and the above principles, he believed that England would never recapture her former "dignity and happiness." In his diary for June 2, 1851, he wrote that his prayer was that he might do the will of God and serve his own generation as David had done.

Some might think that his adherence to the basic principles of faith and love in the Christian's life and service might have led Shaftesbury to think that social reform could create a Utopia in England. It was his strong belief in the imminent coming of Christ that kept him from any false optimism as to the outcome of his work. He believed that only the coming of Christ and His rule upon earth would eradicate evil. He told his biographer Hodder that belief in the doctrine of the Second Advent of Christ had been "a moving principle" in his life and that he saw everything as "subordinate to this one great event." This event was so important to him that he had the words "Even so come, Lord Jesus" in the original Greek printed on the flaps of all his envelopes. He was conscious of the fact that the age of grace seemed to be drawing to a close even in his day. The return of the Lord Jesus Christ was to him the only final remedy for the "mass of misery" in the world.

He believed that the Jews would return to their own land before the coming of Christ would take place. Consequently he watched the turn of diplomatic events in the Near East with interest and, whenever opportunity presented itself, used his influence to promote the return of Jews to Palestine so that the way would be open for the return of Christ. The words, "Oh, pray for the peace of Jerusalem!" were engraved on the ring which he always wore on his right hand. He believed that his departed loved ones would return with Christ.

All human efforts at reform were thus relative to Christ's

coming and, even though springing from Christian love, such efforts could never achieve a Christian Utopia in England or any other land. Life should be a preparation of man's heart for the coming of Christ. He wrote in his diary for September 27, 1847, that he delighted in his belief that Christ would personally reign on earth and that he could not understand the Scriptures in any other way. Only the Second Coming would set a limit to the sins and future sufferings of mankind. According to an entry in his diary for Good Friday, April 6, 1849, he did not believe that the world was any better in his day than the day Christ died on Calvary. After the gospel had been preached in all nations—to him China and Japan were the last areas to be reached—the return of Christ might be expected. Again and again in his writings words of prayer for the immediate coming of Christ occurred. He firmly believed that not human agency but the coming of Christ alone would save the world.

The Biblical principles of faith, love and hope inspired all of his numerous activities for the poor and oppressed from the day that his dismay at the callous treatment of the dead body of a poor man by his drunken friends led him, while still a schoolboy, to dedicate himself to God to aid the poor and oppressed of England. The working people of England sensed this love in him. One worker-mourner after his death said that God knew Shaftesbury loved the workers and they him, and that the workers would never see his like again.

There was little difference between the views of Shaftesbury, Wilberforce or Wesley except that the latter two did not put quite so much emphasis on the Second Advent of Christ as Shaftesbury did. All of them upheld the integrity of Scripture as the sure record which pointed men to the cross where they might find salvation by faith. Love of God would then inspire their hearts to glorify God by service to men in society.

Chapter V

SAINTS AND SOCIETY IN THE TWENTIETH CENTURY

THE PREVIOUS ACCOUNTS of the source, scope and spirit of social activity constitute an adequate case study to provide empirical historical principles to help Evangelicals relate Biblical faith and ethics to the problems of society in our day without falling into the errors of the social gospel. In them the awakened conscience of Evangelicals can find help in assessing the spirit, strategy and scope of their social responsibilities. Many voices call for attention to their particular panaceas for the ills that beset the human race, and many have succumbed to these faulty solutions. Fear of the humanistic, sometimes socialistic, social gospel of the Liberals and the battle to retain doctrinal purity have long kept Evangelicals from giving attention to this practical aspect of Christianity.

From the second century there have been those who advocated a policy of *retreat* from participation in society or depreciated any attempt to deal with its ills on the ground that the world would become increasingly evil and apostate prior to the coming of Christ. Christ was thought to be in opposition to culture. In view of this the responsibility of the Christian was limited to the salvation of his own soul, to ministering to social need among believers, and to preaching judgment upon a sinful world. Such was the viewpoint of

Montanus and his followers in the middle of the second century. They retired to Pepuza in Phrygia to await the coming of Christ to set up His kingdom there. They believed Christ would give them a favored position as administrators in that kingdom. Tertullian, attracted to the teaching of Montanus, also advocated complete separation from the social order of the day.

This approach has been used by some Evangelicals in our day. The writer remembers a Christian who refused to stand for a local office on the ground that evil would only become worse till Christ came, even though it was apparent that his reputation for integrity and firmness was exactly what was needed to clean up the local situation. Paul's reminder in Romans 14:7 that no one is completely independent of others and that social isolation is impossible and unscriptural is a rebuke to this viewpoint.

Those Evangelicals who retreat from involvement in the problems of society find that some of those in the neo-orthodox camp take a similar position for a different reason. Karl Barth believes that society is under the influence of universal sin and that God does not interfere in history except as the individual soul is confronted with the claims of Christ in the Bible by the Holy Spirit. Consequently, he believes, there is little use in the Christian's seeking to modify a transitory historical order by any social activity for the welfare of men. For him "the care of the world is not the care of the church." This viewpoint clashed with that of the activism of the American religious leaders at Amsterdam in 1948 when the World Council of Churches came into being.

Both Evangelicals and neo-orthodox who hold such a view should remember that Christianity is practical, ethical and social as well as personal and doctrinal. While we agree with Shaftesbury that only the supernatural intervention of Christ in His Second Advent will cleanse the world of evil, we should remember as he did that the Christian has the responsibility of manifesting love to his fellows by occupying in whatever scriptural way is open until Christ does return. The Christian may be saved out of the culture of his day, but he still lives in that culture and must remember that Christ in His prayer in John 17:15 prayed that the Christian might be kept *in* the world. Those who retreat from involvement in society really deny in effect that Christ is the Lord of history and forget that in the present the forces of evil only reign over the earth permissively until the maturing of the divine plans for the earth and man. Separation from the world should be spiritual rather than physical.

Others advocate a *revolution* to change society because they believe that man is good and perfectible and that, if the evil environmental influences are changed by force, society can move toward Utopia. Such is the view of the socialistic followers of Karl Marx. The main ideas behind their activities were developed by Karl Marx and Friedrich Engels in the *Communist Manifesto,* published in 1848. For them matter in motion is the only reality. Because of this basic premise they are convinced that the class which controls the forces of production can mold society in its image so that all institutions, even religion, will reflect the basic philosophy of that class. Because of this, class conflict will emerge as the exploited seek to get control of society and remake it in their class image. The workers will seize power in an economic crisis or in war. After a temporary rule by the dictatorship of the proletariat, until the forces of capitalism are subdued, the state will wither away, and a classless society will emerge. In it each will produce according to his ability and receive remuneration according to his needs. This system has appealed to many since its inception over a hundred years ago. Efforts were made in socialist uprisings in France in 1848 and 1871 to put this ideology into practice. Success was withheld from the socialists, however, until the Communists seized control in Russia in November, 1917. Since that time, at least one-third of the world's population has come under the control of this system which simply sets up a new set of masters and exploiters who plunder the helpless masses under their rule of force. Milovan Djilas, a chastened Communist, who realized the evil implications of Communism, developed this thesis ably in his book, *The New Class* (New York: Frederick A. Praeger, 1957).

Communists and most Socialists are atheistic and hostile to religion. Their millennium is purely earthly, to be achieved by human effort. In the struggle, the inexorable forces of history, they think, are on their side. Revolution to set up a communistic order or even an evolutionary democratic development to a socialist order, such as the Labor Party of England has tried to achieve, can, according to them, cope with the problem of human sin. Socialists and Communists are too much under the spell of the optimistic eighteenth-century thinkers. These thinkers proclaimed the goodness and perfectibility of man, who could by the use of reason and science achieve Utopia. Such attempts will always deny or be a perversion of the Christian approach to social problems, even though the Scriptures may be wrested by such people to find support for their ideas. The writer remembers how several years ago a Communist sought in a discussion to gain the support of the Bible for his system by pointing to the temporary voluntary communalism of Acts 4 as the forerunner of the ideas of Karl Marx.

Still others advocate the *reformation* of society by education and democratic social action. They hope to correct the evils of society and thereby bring the kingdom of God on earth. Proponents of this viewpoint in England were Charles Kingsley and his followers, the Christian Socialists, and in America the followers of Walter Rauschenbusch. These people would link Christ with culture.

Walter Rauschenbusch (1861-1918), a Baptist clergyman who was for many years professor of church history in Roch-

Saints and Society in the Twentieth Century 137

ester Seminary in Rochester, New York, confused the social order with the kingdom of God. His main religious idea was the bringing of the kingdom of God to earth. For him the establishment of the kingdom was the main hope for the redemption of the collective life of humanity, just as eternal life through regeneration by Christ was the main hope for the individual. He owed much to the theologian Ritschl who had emphasized the community as the area of redemptive action instead of the individual life.

Rauschenbusch and his followers developed what became known as the social gospel. They approached the problems of society from the institutional, social and external viewpoint. Sin was to them more external, corporate and social than internal, personal, subjective and individual. It was looked upon as physical privation created by an environment hostile to the institutions of the family, church, state and economic order. This almost Pelagian view of sin held by Rauschenbusch denied the Biblical approach to sin as internal, subjective and personal as set forth in such Scriptures are Jeremiah 17:9; Mark 7:14-15, 21-23; Romans 3:23; 14; 23; James 4:11; and I John 3:4. Because he believed that social sin was primarily environmental, Rauschenbusch was hopeful that the social order could be christianized by democratic action in the family, the church, the state and the economic order.

This defective view of sin and the ignoring of the activity of a personal devil (Eph. 2:1-4) was buttressed by an unbiblical eschatology. He thought that human democratic procedures could develop an increasingly perfect order of society until Christ would return to a world which the church had, through an evolutionary democratic process, prepared to be His kingdom. This optimistic, postmillennial eschatology runs counter to the brute facts of modern history. Recent events, such as two world wars, in the second of which genocide, the attempt to wipe out a nation, was practiced, reveal the presence of the demonic in man. Even with the best of will men cannot make real social progress apart from a spiritual dynamic. The atonement of Christ provides this for the individual and for his ethical system. The idea that man will be good and do the good if he but knows the good is an error as old as Socrates. Paul points out in Romans 7 that in his life there was a gap between knowing the good and carrying it out in daily life. Moral idealism, based on the fatherhood of God and the brotherhood of man, is noble but useless if it lacks the dynamic of the cross. An electric light can only give light if power is brought to it from another source. Too often these ideas have only resulted in high-sounding pronouncement of principles by small groups of clergy out of touch with those whom they claim to represent.

Only the approach that one might categorize as *renovation* can meet the situation. Luther believed that works were useless to justify men before God, but after he became a Christian, he believed a man should "be useful to others" and in all his doings consider the need and profit of his neighbor first. The individual must be transformed before one can expect any change in society through his influence. Regeneration must come before reform of society. Only thus can sin which alienates men from God be dealt with. The evangelical reformers we have studied thought or did little about the ills of society before they became Christians. The empirical historical data concerning their faith and work which we have considered forms the background of practice against which one can depict an approach to an evangelical and scriptural view of the Christian's responsibility to the social order in which he lives. The Gospel has a horizontal orientation of love to man to balance the vertical orientation of faith in Christ, who brings one into saving relationship with God. Truth is in order to goodness, and a passion for souls and social zeal can be combined. Only with such a

Saints and Society in the Twentieth Century 139

foundation can a Christian become useful in his society as he seeks to bring the transforming influence of Christ to bear upon his culture.

I. THE SPIRIT OF EVANGELICAL SOCIAL ACTIVITY

The discussion in the previous chapter of the spirit which moved the reformers of the nineteenth century to express their faith in service to the society of their day offers a clue to a positive and dynamic approach on the part of contemporary Evangelicals to the social problems of our own day. The first element in the approach of nineteenth century Evangelicals was faith in the Living Word, who is the subject of the Written Word. The Bible was to them the infallible rule for faith and life, for the expression of love in service to their fellow and, especially in the case of Shaftesbury, for the relation of life in the present to the future coming of Christ. They did not become too optimistic concerning the chances of man's creating a Utopia nor did they become so pessimistic that they would not even try to express their faith in service to their society. Ethics based on love must rest upon faith in a Redeemer in the past and hope for One to cleanse the earth supernaturally in the future.

The empirical historical success of their principles would seem to demonstrate that they were on solid ground with their particular philosophy. In addition, any fair examination of the New Testament will reinforce the correctness of their approach. Thus the Evangelical has an example which is scriptural and which has been empirically verified in human history. Perhaps the best summary occurs in the writings of Paul, where he asserts the primacy of faith, love, and hope (I Cor. 13:13; I Thess. 1:3, cf. 9, 10; Col. 1:4, 5). These three elements recur often in the Scriptures in one form or another.

A. Faith

Discussion of this point involves a consideration of the *kerygma* or preaching of the New Testament church. Man must first of all be related vertically to God. In this process of conversion or the experience of justification by faith, attention must be given to the place of the Bible. Paul in Romans 10:17 writes that "faith cometh by hearing, and hearing by the word of God." The history of revival has ever been the story of a return to God through the agency of His Word. There will be little dynamic in any system that minimizes the importance of the Word of God or denies its validity in favor of a system of criticism which merely reduces it to the level of any other book of history.

That the Bible has a unique place in the creation of saving faith is evident in Paul's practice in Acts 17:2, 3 and in his thought in I Corinthians 15:3, 4. According to him, the Scriptures declare that Christ died and rose again to free man from sin. Any careful study of the practice of the apostles, as revealed in the Book of Acts, will show that the proclamation of salvation by faith in the Messiah, who was foretold by the prophets and who died and rose again that man might be saved, was the basic content of their *kerygma*. When Paul wrote to Timothy, he told Timothy that it had been the Scriptures, which he had been taught from his youth, that had made him wise unto salvation by faith in Christ (II Tim. 3:15).

The personal orientation of the human soul to God must be the starting point if the principles which govern our participation in service in the social order are not to be faulty in their beginning. There can be no vital social impact of Christian significance without a saving faith in Christ, which guarantees salvation of the soul (I Peter 1:9).

The social reformers, whose work has been considered, all had experience of regeneration by the Spirit of God on the ground of Christ's work on the cross. Every one of them looked on this as the starting point of their loving service to their fellows. Only through coming in penitent faith to the cross can one know anything of the mind of Christ (Phil. 2: 5) for the order in which we live.

The importance of Christ the living Word as a foundation for life is pointed out by the written Word (I Cor. 3:11). From this it follows that the main task of the Christian and the Church is to be "light" (Matt. 5:14) which points to the "Light," our Lord Jesus Christ. It will be remembered that, in addition to the Evangelicals' enthusiasm for the freeing of the slaves and for better conditions for the workers of England, they also supported every activity to bring men to Christ and used every means made possible by technological progress to speed that end. It was they who opened India to missions in 1813 after the British East India Company had been there for over 200 years without a thought of, nay, even opposing, the preaching of the Gospel to the natives. It was they who were the originators of the British and Foreign Bible Society, which was to bring the written Word to men in order that they might come to know the living Word. It is at this point that the great evangelists, from Wesley, Whitefield, Edwards, Finney and Moody to Billy Graham, find the justification for expending their energies in a passionate evangelism. Man is a sinner who is totally depraved and unable to help himself but whose soul is of infinite value to a God who does not will that any man should perish. It was God's love for helpless, sinful man that led Him to send His beloved Son as Saviour (John 3:16; Rom. 5:8).

It is in this assertion that the Jewish-Christian heritage of the western civilization differs from its Greco-Roman heritage in their common assertion that man is a personality worthy of dignified treatment. The ancient classical philosophers believed that human personality was of great value and was to be respected because man was a rational creature. This was back of the thinking of the eighteenth century rationalists and the nineteenth century rationalistic reformers, such as Jeremy Bentham and John Stuart Mill. In contrast, both the Old and New Testaments assert that man is a living soul of infinite value to God and, therefore, a creature of dignity because he is either a potential or an actual son of God through faith in Christ. It is exactly at this point that the modern totalitarian systems deny any dignity and individuality to man. To such systems, man is merely a means to the end, the preservation and continuance of the life of the state, and is to be manipulated to that end by radio, television, the press and social pressure.

The Christian who is interested in the social implications of the Gospel should never forget these facts. Social activity of the Christian is always a result and a means but never an end in itself. Social reform in the Christian sense must always start with the individual by seeking to bring him into a saving relationship to Christ by which he becomes a new creature (II Cor. 5:17). Only then can he act in society in any dynamic fashion. In his preoccupation with the supposed social nature of sin, Rauschenbusch and his followers forgot that corporate or institutional manifestations of sin stem from the activities of Satan or individual men whether they be in the social, economic or political spheres.

Interest in the social implications of the Gospel must never be permitted to blind the Evangelical to the fact that the only commission Christ gave the Church in the synoptic Gospels was to go "into all the world and preach the gospel" (Matt. 28:18-20; Acts 1:8; Acts 17:2, 3; I Cor. 15:1, 3, 4). It was to this *kerygma* that the Church, as described in the Book of Acts, addressed itself. That the Messiah had come to give through His death salvation to those who believe on Him was the major thrust of their preaching. The order is from the Written Word to the Living Word before one becomes concerned about the social order. Peter's message on the day of Pentecost was repentance and faith in Christ. The redemptive work of the Cross is the foundation for ethics. Harry Emerson Fosdick, in his autobiographical book, *The Living of These Days*[1], confessed that, if he started with social problems, he found that only superior individuals might cope with social disorder. But if he started with a personal gospel, the evils of society affecting persons forced him to elaborate a social gospel. Faith is fundamental to personal and social ethics, and morality is the result of the vision of God in Christ.

B. LOVE

If the preaching of salvation by faith in Christ to souls of infinite value to God is the primary task of the Christian, his next task is the horizontal manifestation of *agape* or love. Love is the flower that faith in Christ produces. The Christian, who in the first instance is "light" to point the world to the Light, is also to be "salt" to the social order. The acceptance of the proclamation of the *kerygma* should result in *agape* and *diakonia*, namely, love and service. Religion, which up to this point has been vertical and individual, now becomes horizontal and social.

Like Wesley, the Evangelical knows no religion that is solitary. Because he has love to God through faith in Christ this love manifests itself horizontally on earth in service to the needs of others. Christ, who urged us to love God with all the intensity of our being, also urged us to love our neighbor as ourselves (Matt. 22:37-39; Deut. 6:5). This love is even to be extended to our enemies (Rom. 12:19-21). His commandment to believe on His Son is followed by His commandment to love one another (I John 3:23, 24; Lev. 19:18). If we love Him, we will want to keep all His commandments (John 15:17). The man who has been confronted by Christ and who has accepted His claims upon his life will find that the Gospel will exercise control in every

---
[1] New York: Harper & Brothers, 1956, pp. 279, 280.

area of his life. Truth is always in order to goodness in the life; faith begets love and to love is to serve. After all, the Gospel is for the whole man (I Thess. 5:23) in order that men might become free in every aspect of their personalities (John 8:32). Ethics for the Christian is rooted in faith in and love to a Person and not merely adherence to abstract or propositional principles (Phil. 4:13).

The manifestation of love in service involves the consideration of certain principles. Witness to the saving grace of Christ might involve witnessing by deeds as well as by word. Scripture makes it clear that the Christian is a member of two societies, the heavenly commonwealth (Phil. 3:20) and the world in which he finds himself as a physical soulish being. He lives in a community as a member of the City of Earth as well as being a part of the spiritual City of God. So he has an obligation to live out his Christianity practically in his social context. It is through the believer that the Lordship of Christ is made manifest in society.

It should be clear, however, from the previous historical study and Scripture that this activity in society does not involve the church as an organization becoming a mere pressure group. The clergy through preaching and teaching make known the implications of the Scripture so that the Christian layman, as a member of the family, the educational system, the economic and the political order, may apply these principles in daily life as a Christian citizen. When the Church as an organization has interfered in society, it has lost its spiritual nature and become an institution which claimed the right to temporal control. It has then encroached upon the God-delegated sphere of state power.

The Christian in expressing this love horizontally to his fellows would make no mistake in following the pattern which Paul has set down in Galatians 6:10. Paul urges us to do good to all men but especially to them who are of like faith. The first expression of Christian stewardship is within

Saints and Society in the Twentieth Century 145

the circle of believers. The needs in other than spiritual spheres of those who hold the "common faith" have a legitimate claim upon the efforts and resources of the Christian. Then the principle of stewardship is to be applied to those who have not had the experience of faith in Christ.

Love, as a principle actuating the Christian in the social sphere, may lead him, as he applies the principles which the church teaches, to serve as a critic of society. This is a part of his responsibility as the "salt" (Matt. 5:12) of society. He should be aware of the evils in any given social order and offer criticism where it is needed in order to hold human action up to the high standard of the Word of God. The Christian will seek first to bring to the light of the Bible individuals in the groups responsible for social evil so that they might be won to Christ and have their consciences sensitized to the will of God. Socially organized evil and the idolatry of institutions, such as the state, are simply the social manifestation of individual sin.

Mere criticism of social evil is not enough. The Christian citizen will seek action in whatever way is legitimate to correct the evils by co-operation with those who are also conscious of the evil. In this way the Christian will help to turn the world, which has inverted moral values, right side up.

In all his activity he avoids the negative function which the critic of the social order often takes. Marx wanted to destroy the old society and to make a new world. He wanted to break completely with the past and to destroy it. The Christian seeks to preserve that which is good in society and to remove only that which is defective, sinful or opposed to the general good. He would make the principles of absolute scriptural ethics operative in society insofar as it is possible. This involves the recognition that lasting moral improvement of society must be actuated by a spiritual dynamic. Only as men come to Christ can there be any real improvement in life. Reformation is always the result of repentance and regeneration. Social action in the Christian sense is an outcome of faith.

C. HOPE

Another essential element in any approach to an evangelical conception of how the Christian is to relate himself to his social order involves a Christian hope. This will enable him to avoid the twin dangers of false utopianism and passivity in the presence of individual evil in society. Apart from God one might, like the German philosopher of history, Oswald Spengler, feel that society is doomed to destruction at its own hands. The Christian with a hope of the Second Coming of Christ as the consummation of history can never take this attitude of despair.

Even though one is a child of God, he might, like the Montanists, Tertullian and the medieval monks, feel that the earth is ripening for the judgment of God and that society will wax worse and worse until it is finally judged at the end of the age. In that case the salvation of his own soul and a personal preparation for the coming of Christ is the Christian's only duty. This view is held by some evangelical Christians. They refuse to recognize that the Christian has the duty of occupying until the coming of Christ by loving service to his fellows within the context of the social order. They see the evil but limit the power of God to work through them in dealing with it. Their pessimism leads them rather to passivity in the social expression of their Christian faith than to patient application of Christian principles in society while awaiting Christ's coming.

At the same time the hope of Christ's return to earth keeps the Evangelical from being optimistic to the point of refusing to face the reality, as do those who hold to the social gospel, that man can never eradicate sin totally from earth by human effort. The Evangelical believes that a new world order will never come by an evolutionary process in the hands of men. Only the cataclysmic return of Christ will finally bring into being a new order on earth (II Peter 3:11-15). Individual salvation occurs in the present age, but social salvation can only be consummated at Christ's coming by His power. The Christian will not be expecting a Utopia through human effort as Karl Marx and theological Liberals have done. Christ's teaching that the tares and wheat grow together and that the good and bad fish are in the net (Matt. 13:24-30, 36-43, 47-51) until the end of the age, when Christ appears, will be kept in mind. This view will inject realism into the Christian's efforts in the social order to realize partially the ethics of Christianity.

The true Christian who seeks to promote righteousness in the social order will surrender neither to pessimism nor passivity in the face of entrenched evil nor will he have an unrealistic hope that a perfect social order can be achieved. That can come only with the return of Christ and His supernatural, cataclysmic intervention in the affairs of men. The millennial kingdom of Biblical prophecy will not come through human effort. The "D-Day" of Calvary guarantees Christ's final victory at His coming. Instead, the Christian will seek to occupy by the expression of love in service while awaiting the imminent return of Christ. This effort is made valid by the idea that, while man will never achieve final perfect order in his society by his own efforts, the Christian has the responsibility of living out the ethical implications of the Gospel in every segment of his life. While he patiently awaits and hopefully watches, he will be working to the ends of the conversion of souls and the application of Christian ethics to his life in society. While we can never finally capture culture for Christ, it is our task to live as Christian citizens by applying the Gospel in every area that "our whole spirit and soul and body may be preserved blameless unto the coming of Christ" (I Thess. 5:23).

Such was the hope that kept Shaftesbury at the task in his

day of expressing his faith by a love which sought the glory of God and the good of his fellows. He believed this was a calling from God to himself as a Christian. Faith, hope and love are the essential elements that must form the foundation for the activity of the Christian while he seeks prayerfully as an individual to co-operate with others in order to make his faith practical and relevant to the problems of his day in the social order. Such a conception of the Christian's relation to society will help him to avoid an attitude of indifference to a sinful passing world brought on by an attitude of passively waiting Christ's coming or a neo-monastic retreat from society.

II. THE STRATEGY OF EVANGELICAL SOCIAL ACTIVITY

Even a superficial study of the activities of the men we have been considering reveals that they used a definite strategy and tactics to carry out their mission of loving service in the social order. In fact the anti-slavery movement was the first successful propagandist agitation of the type that has become in our day highly refined techniques of propaganda. There is some evidence that later organizations, such as labor unions, who had in so many cases Methodist lay ministers as their leaders, adapted many of the techniques of the Evangelicals for their purposes. The Evangelicals pioneered new methods of agitating and of educating public opinion.

A. Securing the Facts

Christ's statement to the effect that knowledge of the truth will bring freedom (John 8:32) seems to summarize very well the first and very important aspect of the activities of the Evangelicals in social reform. They all had a healthy respect for the power of truth to mold a public opinion that would force action. They spent much time and money in getting the facts to lay before the people. They were never satisfied to present their case either to the public or to Parliament until they were sure that their case was airtight. They realized that lack of correct facts might lose their case. This respect for facts can be illustrated repeatedly in their activities.

When Granville Sharp was trying to get the courts of England to outlaw slavery in England by judicial decision, even though he was not a lawyer, he spent two years studying the law of England to see if he could find a precedent that would make the holding of slaves impossible in England. He did this in spite of the advice of his own lawyers who told him that slaves were property and that nothing could be done for them. The persistent work of Sharp, a mere layman in the legal field, confounded the legal minds of England and freed 14,000 slaves. This Christian layman, who was convinced from the study of his Bible that slavery was unscriptural, had won his case on the basis of hard facts procured by long, patient, painstaking effort.

When Wilberforce in 1790 managed to get a Select Committee of the House of Commons to examine evidence concerning the slave trade, Thomas Clarkson provided most of the anti-slavery evidence. A friend told Clarkson of a sailor who had been in Africa and who knew how slaves were procured.[1] Even though he did not have the man's name, Clarkson decided to find him. He boarded 160 vessels at Deptford, 60 at Woolwich, Sheerness and Chatham and 40 at Plymouth. When he boarded the 317th ship, the *Melampus,* at Plymouth, he found his sailor, whose name until that time he had not known. The sailor, Isaac Parker, gave invaluable evidence concerning the techniques of obtaining slaves. Again the patient search for factual information to create a solid case was helpful to Wilberforce in finally bringing about in 1807 the abolition of the slave trade by Englishmen.

---

[1] Though the slave trade had been an important part of English commerce since 1562, little was known about the trade by those who were not directly engaged in it.

Zachary Macaulay's years on a slave plantation in the West Indies had given him a first-hand acquaintance with slavery on the plantation. His sojourn in Sierra Leone had given him first-hand information on how slaves were procured. When ill and worn-out by his arduous labor as governor of the freed slave colony of Sierra Leone, he was asked to return to England in 1795 to report to the directors of the company and to recuperate. He gave up direct passage in a clean, comfortable ship to England. Instead he took passage in a slave-ship, which was bound for Barbados with a cargo of slaves, in order that he might see for himself the horrors of the Middle Passage between Africa and the colonies in America. His cabin was just over the slave hold where there were 170 male and 70 female slaves. He commented that the smell was "almost beyond endurance" and the noise of the slaves' moans "excessive." This trip took from May 6 to 29. From Barbados he went to England. All this information he later supplemented by careful study between 1823 and 1833. He became as valuable an aid to Buxton, the leader in the House, as Clarkson had been formerly to Wilberforce in the securing of authentic information. It is little wonder that when any of the abolitionists wanted information on slavery they would jokingly say "look it up in Macaulay."

Shaftesbury had just as much respect for facts as the abolitionists and would present no case in Parliament on behalf of the workers of England unless he was sure he had complete and accurate information which his opponents could not gainsay. The length to which he went to secure information is revealed by an incident in July, 1848. He thought that migration to the colonies might give some of the thieves of London a chance to have a new start in different surroundings. He asked a London city missionary, Thomas Jackson, to put him in touch with thieves so he could meet with them to talk his project over. Forty thieves then wrote letters to Shaftesbury concerning the meeting. Accompanied by Jackson this titled gentleman on July 27 met with an assembly of 400 thieves of various kinds. Shaftesbury took the chair and opened the meeting with devotions. After a period of mutual questioning and answers, he found that all the men were unhappy with the life which they were leading and would welcome a chance to migrate and start life anew in one of the colonies. As a result, he was able to get financial aid to help many to emigrate. He later received many letters of gratitude from reformed thieves who had made a new start on an honest life in Canada or Australia. In seeking information Shaftesbury did not hesitate to visit slums, to go down into dirty, dangerous mines and to sleep overnight in lodging-houses infested with vermin. Thus he could speak with authority when he wanted action on behalf of the poor and oppressed.

B. TECHNIQUES TO CREATE CHRISTIAN PUBLIC OPINION

Facts or information alone would not have been enough if the evangelical reformers had not known how to publicize the facts in order to create an informed public opinion that would demand democratic action to correct the evils exposed. Several devices were developed to publicize their case so that the conscience of the Christian public would be sensitized and aroused to demand action wherever it was needed. In 1831, George Stephen formed "The Agency Committee" to arrange for public meetings all over England, to arrange for lecturers to speak to these meetings and to promote the signing of petitions demanding an end of slavery in the British Empire. Part of Buxton's success in pushing the Emancipation Act through Parliament in 1833 was the result of the activities of this committee which gave the people the facts, urged them to act and provided the means for action. William Wilberforce and others wrote letters to the editor of *The Times* of London in order to get the facts of their case before the public. Billboards with factual messages were put up to stimulate interest and action. The annual mass meetings of missionary societies at Exeter became an excellent sounding board for those seeking reform. By his speeches at Exeter Hall meetings of the London Missionary Society, John Philip was able to arouse the Christian public to the need of the Cape Colored for protection. Wilberforce's campaign to abolish the slave trade was helped by the publication of Cowper's Poem, "The Negro's Complaint." It was printed on good paper and circulated in fashionable circles. When it was later set to music, it became a popular music-hall ballad. Elizabeth Barrett Browning's "Song of the Shirt" helped Shaftesbury's efforts on behalf of the workers in textile mills. The Quaker maker of fine china, Josiah Wedgwood, had a lovely blue and white cameo made picturing a kneeling Negro with hands clasped and upraised. The words "Am I not a man and a brother?" were below the picture. This was used on brooches, hairpins and snuff boxes which became fashionable.

From Sharp to Wilberforce all the leaders were experts in writing pamphlets. Clarkson and Macaulay digested the information concerning slavery and put it into cheap, well-written pamphlets for public consumption. In this regard, perhaps without knowledge on their part, they were following the pattern of the seventeenth-century English Puritans who wrote political pamphlets to help them in their struggle to limit the power of the English king.

Boycotts of slave-grown products, such as sugar from the West Indies, proved to be a good weapon to get the public aroused concerning the need to end slavery. Clarkson claimed in 1792 that 300,000 stopped using sugar produced in the British West Indies.

The abolitionists also published their own magazines. From 1802 until 1816 the *Christian Observer* with Zachary Macaulay as editor was published to keep its subscribers informed regarding the state of the struggle, to give them facts

Saints and Society in the Twentieth Century 153

and to urge them to action. *The Anti-Slavery Reporter* became the main organ of the forces seeking abolition of slavery in the British Empire between 1823 and 1833.

C. METHODS TO OBTAIN ACTION

After securing the facts and getting them to the people, the abolitionists faced the task of getting action on their demands. The cell idea of John Wesley's class meeting, where a band of about twelve helped one another to develop spiritually, became the nucleus for local corresponding societies to raise money, to stir up sentiment and to demand action on the reformer's program. Thomas Clarkson in 1806 organized societies all over England to create the public demand which brought about the act abolishing the slave trade in 1807.

The annual meetings of missionary societies at Exeter Hall were also used to secure the passage of resolutions and to obtain signatures on petitions demanding Parliamentary action. A great anti-slavery meeting was held in London in 1833 with the venerable Clarkson in the chair.

In addition to the raising of funds to carry on their publicity campaign, other results came out of the meetings described above. People were urged to vote for legislators who would promise action on the desired bills. In 1806, when it seemed as if Wilberforce might lose his seat, thirteen influential Methodists of York sent out a letter over their signature urging that the Methodists support Wilberforce by their vote. Resolutions were also passed by local public rallies, and petitions were circulated. In 1792 nearly 229,000 names on petitions urging the banning of the slave trade by Englishmen came to Parliament. In 1813, Wilberforce and his followers had the support of over 800 large petitions asking that the British government act to ban the slave trade by Europeans at the Congress of Vienna which sought to make a settlement in Europe after the long period of war from 1792.

Saints and Society

When Wilberforce and his friends successfully got the charter of the British East India Company changed to admit missionaries to India in 1813, they had the support of 837 petitions with a total of over 500,000 names. Of 354,000 names of Dissenters on petitions in 1833 supporting Buxton's demands for the abolition of slavery in the British Empire, 224,000 were those of Methodists.

In their work the Evangelicals of the Anglican Church welcomed the support not only of Dissenters but also that of the rationalistic Utilitarians. Bentham, who supported the Evangelicals' work of abolition, is credited with the remark that if being an anti-slavist made one a saint, saintship was for him. The Evangelicals wanted reform because men were spiritual beings who were actual or potential sons of God, while Bentham and his followers wanted reform because men had dignity as rational creatures. Bentham emphasized reason and utility based on the greatest good to the greatest number. As long as the efforts of the Utilitarians were directed to the good of men, the Evangelicals would co-operate with them temporarily for a common good end without in any way giving up their religious principles. Evangelicals and rationalistic humanitarians co-operated in the common service of humanity.

These men did not neglect prayer. The spirit of prayer can be sensed in their letters, diaries and journals. In the fight to end slavery in the British Empire, Buxton in 1833 called on the church for a day of prayer to this end. Their efforts were of little avail, they believed, without prayer to invoke the blessing and power of God in their work (Eph. 1:19-22; 3:20).

This consideration of the techniques by which the Evangelicals brought faith, love and hope to bear on the problems of society shows that they did not substitute spirituality or oratory for self-sacrificing hard work in order to have authenticated facts to support their case. They used every possible

Saints and Society in the Twentieth Century 155

legitimate means to educate the public, especially the Christian public of England, in order to create a Christian public opinion. Then by the vote, resolution and petitions, and by speeches by leaders in Parliament, they focused this public opinion on the issue so as to secure necessary legislation to correct the evil. All of these endeavors were undergirded by prayer.

Surely with the new knowledge of the art of public persuasion which psychology has made known, with the many available organs for forming public opinion, and with democratic privileges to obtain action in the halls of legislation, Evangelicals of our day could have greater impact as Christian citizens than they do in the support of Christian principles in legislation to deal with social problems. The spirit and the strategy of Evangelicals are as valid today for dynamic and technique in dealing with the problems of society as they were in the days of Wilberforce and Shaftesbury.

III. THE SCOPE OF EVANGELICAL SOCIAL ACTIVITY

While one must remember that the basic task of the Christian, as enunciated in the Great Commission, is the proclamation of the Gospel, one must also remember that He coupled faith with the expression of love to those around us (I John 3:23). The New Testament knows nothing of the dichotomy which some Christians have set up between their lives as Christians and their participation or, more often, nonparticipation in the social order. Paul tells us that every created thing is good and is to be accepted with thanksgiving (I Tim. 4:4). He had no false distinction between that which is sacred and that which is secular. All creation is from the hand of God and is finally to be brought under the influence of Christ at His Coming.

Paul and John agree in asserting that the order in which the social activity of the Christian is to be expressed is first

156   *Saints and Society*

in the circle of believers, after which all men are included (Gal. 6:10; I John 3:14, 23). This principle of the expression of Christian love in social action to the believer and then to the unbeliever means that the Christian will be interested in the basic institutions of society. These are the family (the unit of society instituted by God subsequent to the creation of man), the church, and those institutions and activities which are a part of our broader social life. This order of interest may be clarified by a chart:

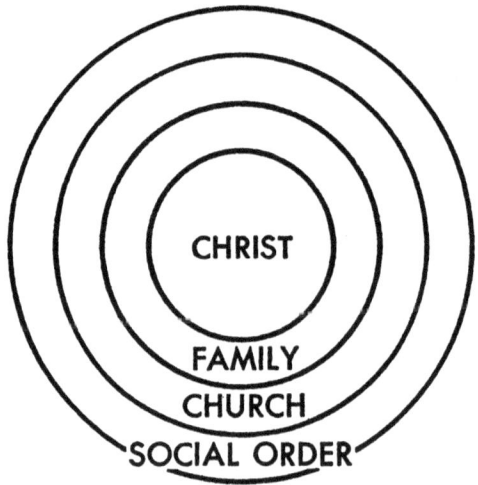

A. FAMILY

Before there can be any organization in society one must take into account the family, an institution coming from the hand of God Himself for the good of man. Three main functions are associated with the origin of the family. God decreed that Adam should have a helpmate in order that he might not be alone (Gen. 2:18-20, 24; Matt. 19:4-6). The moral and spiritual function of the family is to develop love, forbearance and co-operation between husband and wife, and to mold the character of both into the image of Christ. Ideally every marriage should have that degree of fellowship so it will become a perfect picture of the intimate fellowship that exists between Christ and His Church (Eph. 5:22, 33; I Cor. 11:3).

The family is also linked with procreation for the perpetuation of the race (Gen. 1:28; 9:1). Even here man differs from the lower forms of life because procreation is put on a higher spiritual plane as the outcome of a deep mutual love. This view is vastly different from the present sensualizing of love as the basis for marriage.

The family also seems to have the primary responsibility for the education of children, with the major share of the responsibility for that task allocated to the father (Deut. 4:9-10; 11:19; Prov. 4:1; 23:22; Eph. 6:4). Increasingly in our complex, and especially in our suburban society, the father with his time taken up by the demands of business has left that task to the mother. Often she, also a wage-earner, has shifted the major responsibility to the school, which is better fitted to give academic and social education than the basic moral and spiritual training which comes more appropriately by precept and example in the intimate context of the family. Grace before eating, the family altar and family Bible study are important parts of this training. The parents must like Joshua resolve that they and their house will serve the Lord, and the Church must assume responsibility to teach the Christian ideal for the family.

The family faces special dangers in the complex society of modern times. Economic need or the desire for luxuries, which takes the wife out of the home to work, threatens the stability of the home. Drink, sex, divorce, because of a new emphasis upon the right of individualism for the woman and hedonism as the goal for marriage, and delinquency seem to be other dangers.

Liquor will brutalize family life whether the alcoholic tendencies be those of the husband or wife. The wife will neglect the home, and the husband will not accept his responsibility to support the family. Several million Americans have become alcoholics with consequent disaster to their marriages and homes if they have had children. Social drinking, which the beverage industry seems to be promoting by every means of mass persuasion, must bear a share of the responsibility.

Parents who have not resolved their own personal problems will fail to understand their children and, through neglect, overindulgence or arbitrary discipline, will antagonize or in other ways be responsible for inadequate Christian personality development and social controls in their children. More serious, the child's relationship to God will be seriously distorted, and he will express his sinful tendencies in antisocial activities that lead to juvenile delinquency. The reassertion of family discipline along Biblical lines can be a help at this point (Eph. 6:1-4; Col. 3:20, 21).

Often the home and marriage suffer total shipwreck as people under the tensions of modern life deny by divorce the permanent nature of their marriage vows. Pastors with some training in this area and whose own marital relations are sound perhaps could do much more at this point by wise counseling in a Christian scriptural context. Perhaps it is a reflection upon how Christians have failed in this regard that counseling by the courts or by special marriage counselors has so often replaced pastoral counseling in the preservation of marriage.

What can the Christian citizen do to meet this challenge to the basic unit of society? Perhaps he has a responsibility to deal with the problems of obscene literature, television shows and movies. These are some of the media of mass communication which seem to be threatening the stability of the family. A study by the National Association of Evangelicals' Commission on Social Action found that obscene literature was a major concern to ministers related to that organization. This study and the work of other Christian leaders and organizations in church and state resulted in the setting up of the Churchmen's Commission for Decent Publications. Evangelical Christians can support such organizations in their attempt to get action on the local, state and federal level in order to have restrictive legislation passed or to support the strong enforcement of existing laws against pornographic literature. As long as the Christian does nothing, he cannot expect the non-Christian to become disturbed about such things. In this connection he should by practice and by persuasion seek to create a moral atmosphere which will help to bring about the elimination of a double standard of sexual morality which permits men to hold a lower code than women. Christ's standard is single and similar both for men and women.

He can protest as an individual subscriber against liquor advertising in magazines which link drinking with "men of distinction." He can support legislation which will restrict some of the blatant advertising on billboards or through media of mass communication, such as radio and television. Perhaps such advertising could be brought under the pure food and drug act for purposes of control.

Such organizations as the Community Chest and Salvation Army, which exist to meet needs created by the breakdown of the family, might well be supported by the Christian desirous of putting his Christianity into practice, even though he may not always find himself in agreement with their philosophy. For the Evangelical, such organizations as the Evangelical Welfare Agency, which meets the needs of children from broken homes who wind up in the courts, will be most worthy of support.

All of this reminds one of Wilberforce's early efforts to create an organization which would combat immorality and vice. The Christian citizen can do no less than he in carrying out his commission of love to others by fighting anything which threatens the God-given institution of the family.

B. THE CHURCH

While the primary task of the church is to win men to Christ, the Christian is also interested in the relationship of the church as a fellowship of believers to its environment. This particularly involves the principle of importance in democratic society that church and state should be separated and that religion is a private matter rather than a public matter. Few realize that this is a comparatively modern idea. Until the Reformation the principle of a universal religious organization held sway in Western Europe. The Reformation, except for the Anabaptists and Puritan Separatists, who were ahead of their time, did not separate church and state but put the church under the state in most cases and made it a state church. The principle of denominationalism and the separation of church and state so that religion is a private matter is closer to the scriptural idea than a state or universal church. The Constitution of the United States makes it clear that there should be no favored or established church which will be in a position to enforce its tenets upon others or obtain their unwilling support through taxation for church purposes. It will be remembered that it was an evangelical Christian, William E. Gladstone, who, as leader of the British government, was convinced in 1869 that it was unjust to tax the Irish for support of an established Anglican Church when most of them were Roman Catholic. He had the Anglican Church in Ireland disestablished even though he personally had little use for the Roman Catholic system.

On the other hand, separation of the church and state need not involve hostility to the church or religion by the state nor even the neutral attitude which would disassociate the application of Christian principles on the part of the voter and politicians to the affairs of government. Christians should see that the liberties which permit the church to fulfill its primary function of preaching the Gospel meet with no inter-

Saints and Society in the Twentieth Century 161

ference from the state. It was Wilberforce who marshaled the Christian public opinion of England in 1813 so that Parliament would modify the charter of the British East India Company to permit the entrance of missionaries to India in order to proclaim the Gospel to the people of that land. The problem of persecution of Protestants by Roman Catholics should be of interest to Christians so that they, as citizens, through organizations, such as the National Association of Evangelicals, through letters to appropriate legislators and officials can aid those called to preach the Gospel in such lands to have the legal freedom to do it on even terms with other religions. More attention should also be given to the political aims of Roman Catholicism in our land in order to oppose any attempt at securing a favored position in relation to the state.

The Christian citizen will endeavor to uphold the sanctity of the Christian Sunday as a day of rest and worship. This becomes increasingly difficult in an increasingly complex and interdependent society in which some activities must necessarily go on even on Sunday. But he can support any movement which seeks to eliminate unnecessary activities which do not create real worship or recreation. Any society which gives up its day of rest and worship will be bound to come under the influence of secularism. Although admitting that not all business can be brought to a halt, namely, transportation, in a complex interdependent society, he will do his best personally and as a Christian citizen to support anything which will preserve the fast-dwindling sanctity of one day of rest.

One caution should be introduced here. It is important that the church as an organization should not become a mere pressure group in society. Church leaders are fallible and often divided in opinion concerning political and economic matters. All of the reforms of the Evangelicals were carried out by well-informed individual Christian citizens, such as

Wilberforce and Shaftesbury. The clergy felt free, however, to preach on the Biblical principles involved in such issues as slavery, but they acted as individual citizens when they co-operated with the Reformers. This author is of the opinion that this principle is important because, in doing otherwise, the church seeks to dominate the political organs of the state and to break down the principle of a proper separation between church and state. The Puritan preachers delivered election sermons in which they pointed out the relevance of Biblical principles in connection with the men and issues involved. When they and church members voted or acted as officials, however, they acted as Christians who were functioning in their civic capacity. The church has an interest in the relationship of the Bible to political, economic and social issues in order to bring Biblical principles to bear upon the issue. But the effecting of those principles seems to be, on the basis of our historical study, the work of the informed member of the church. He as a conscientious citizen puts these principles into action. The fellowship of believers provides a sense of community which modern industry with its separation of capital and labor and the modern tendency to exalt the state cannot provide. It is in this community that the dynamic of faith, acting in love, is inspired and instructed.

C. SOCIETAL RELATIONSHIPS

1. *Political Responsibilities*

Political responsibilities, or the obligations of the Christian citizen to the state, constitute another area in which the Christian can express his faith socially. It must not be forgotten that Paul and the early Christians lived under a totalitarian state in which they had no franchise to exercise. Yet Paul urges that the Christian fulfill his obligations to the state. If he believed this while living under such brutal totalitarian rulers as Nero, how much more is our responsibility in a democracy where we have the privilege of the vote, office-holding and molding of public opinion by legal means.

Saints and Society in the Twentieth Century 163

This question is especially acute in the twentieth century when the democratic state is under attack by reactionary rightist totalitarian systems, such as Fascism and Nazism, which brought on World War II, and totalitarianism of the left, such as Communism. Perhaps if Christians in those lands had fulfilled their civic functions more effectively there would have been less chance for these systems to rise.

We must recognize the Christian roots of democracy. Classical democracy, which was limited to the aristocratic, more cultured class, was slave-based. Neither the Middle Ages nor the Renaissance gave much attention to the common man. The Christian conception imparts dignity to the individual who is a potential or actual son of God and who is equal to other men in his creation, sinnership, infinite worth to God, in access to the Bible and salvation and in the government of the church. This message was preached by the Reformers.

What are the principles which should govern the state when looked at from the Christian viewpoint? The absolute sovereignty of God as the ultimate moral and spiritual reality from whom all earthly beings and institutions arise and from whom they derive their relative sovereignty is a basic postulate. The state is a God-given, finite means to achieve justice and restrain greed in society, a servant of God and not a master of men. Even pagan states are declared to be under the divine control and moral principles of God by the writers of Old Testament books (see Deut. 32:8; Job 12:23; Ps. 10:16; Isa. 10:5-7; Jer. 27:4-8; Dan. 2:21; Amos 9:7). The statements of the apostle Paul in Romans 13:1, "the powers that be are ordained of God," and of other New Testament writers (I Peter 2:14; John 19:10; Col. 1:16) indicate God's provision of government to establish justice and to promote liberty. This assertion of the origin of the state in the mandate of God refers to the principle of government rather than to the form of government. Christianity cannot be identified with any one political or economic system. Men may use the principle of divine authority wrongly and create by force or subversion a government which is despotic and contrary to the divine will. The government's task is to protect the good and punish the evil under the absolute sovereignty of God. The Christian should by his vote, letters and other influence endeavor to hold the government to a recognition of this principle. If we do not recognize the divine origin of government and the sanction of the moral law, the alternative is a secular philosophy of the state which may find the source of the state in violence and its sanction in force.

That the dignity and worth of the human personality can best be realized in a free society is another principle. Society consists of a plurality of persons, not an organism in which the individual loses his identity. Man is the end; the state is the means. Because of this the state should respect the rights of the individual to life, liberty and property to the extent that these are not used to infringe like rights of others. Because men are equal in the sight of God, they should be equal before the law with favoritism for none. Government is to be by law and not by the whims of men, which pass for law, in a totalitarian state. Private interests will be recognized as legal so long as they do not infringe on the public order and safety. The distinction between public and private and between society and the state, which does not exist in totalitarian states, will permit the free existence of religious, fraternal, political, literary and artistic organizations essential to man's development and creativity.

That the laws of the state, created to protect its existence and the rights of the individual, should be in accord with the laws of God is a third principle. Here the Christian can help to sharpen the conscience of the state. Shaftesbury contended that the politically wrong could never be morally right and that the morally right could never be politically wrong. Our day reveals how demonic the unchecked power of the state can be. Big government, by failing to preserve justice, can destroy democracy as easily as big labor or big business.

Finally, both the governed and governors must be loyal to the will of God in the allocation of spheres of responsibility. The state as a "servant of God" is also answerable to God. Christ pointed out that there were the twin realms of Christ and Caesar (Matt. 22:21; I Peter 2:17). This means that, while the Christian owes loyalty to the state's legitimate demands, there will be a limit to the power of the state. Our obedience to the state is not absolute; it is obedience under God. Peter told the Jewish Sanhedrin that obedience to God took priority over the state when the institutions of the state demanded obedience in areas that were manifestly contrary to the Word of God (Acts 5:29). The Christian is at liberty to resist passively anything which would make him violate the will of God. This principle will oppose the worship of the monolithic state and the communal despotism which is so characteristic of modern totalitarianism.

The Christian will also avoid any scheme for a theocratic perfectionism in the social order which would make him an anarchist seeking to upset the established order so he can create his own order. Desire for such perfectionism led the Anabaptists of Münster in 1535 to create a state in that city which legalized polygamy and the community of property. The same was true of the Mormons after their trek to Salt Lake when they tried to create a state in which polygamy was permitted. The individual as well as the state must submit to the will of God.

Nor should the Christian fall into the error of an irresponsible neutralism or asceticism which considers politics as a dirty business. If it is dirty, perhaps the fault is partly that of the church for permitting it so to degenerate. Government in a democracy usually reflects what the body politic is morally and spiritually. The Evangelicals lifted the moral tone of politics all during the nineteenth century in England and sensitized the public conscience to evils in the body politic until they were reformed.

With these four principles in mind it will be observed that Paul has clearly stated that the main *function* of the state is to make possible the leading "of a quiet and peaceable life in all godliness and honesty" (I Tim. 2:2). This implies freedom from both internal (quiet) and external (peaceable) strife. If the state is God-fearing this ideal might well become a reality.

In return for such privileges and rights the Christian owes certain obligations to the state according to the Bible. First of all, because the state is a governing and not a producing agency, its citizens will insure its continued existence by the payment of taxes necessary to enable it to exist and to fulfill its necessary functions. Paul states the obligation to pay taxes in Romans 13:6, 7. While we should pay our taxes in a democracy, we should also accept the obligation to see that the receipts are put to use in fulfilling proper functions of government as economically and as honestly as possible. Government can only rise as high in the moral scale as the people who make up its civil service. Perhaps in this regard the withholding system of income tax collection is not an unmixed blessing because under it many people are oblivious as to how large a proportion of their income goes to the government and hence less concerned with becoming a part of the public favoring sound economical government. Fiscally irresponsible big government promotes inflation as much as irresponsible big business or big labor.

Respect for the state as an instrument of government for human good is also emphasized by Peter and Paul. This respect will be rendered not only in singing the national anthem or in saluting the flag but also by vote, voice, pen and office-holding if one has the ability. The Christian will

Saints and Society in the Twentieth Century 167

support that candidate, party or policy which puts the common good in the light of Scriptures above personal or group interests. He will prefer that candidate or party which displays moral rectitude and which considers public office a trust from God as well as the people. In these ways one can help to get the type of government and participants in governments whom he can respect. This is especially important because corrupt government leads to public disillusionment with democratic government, which may result in its destruction and replacement by an authoritarian system. In 1956 about forty million adults, many of them Christians, did not take the trouble to vote in the national election for the presidency.

Paul believed also that the Christian has a responsibility to obey the law up to the point where he may be called upon to violate the law of God and his conscience in the fulfillment of obedience. No citizen or group of citizens should ever be permitted to put their personal, sectional, class or group interests above the common good as determined by the principles of government before enunciated. When people seek their own interests, governments become corrupted. Such subordination of the public good to private selfish interest led to the decay of democracy in Greece and Rome and many other democratic states since that time.

The greatest service the Christian can render to the state is to pray for those in authority (I Tim. 2:2). Integrity and information, which are dependent upon religion and education, are necessary to continue a state as a successful unit under good government. Without integrity in the lives both of the governed and the governors the state will not long exist. Prayer will support the development and continuance of such integrity.

Religion also has long supported the idea of education which makes it possible for the person to get the information necessary to make intelligent decisions in a democracy. Any attempt to keep legitimate information or information not essential to real national security secret should meet with the opposition of the Christian. The free flow of knowledge is essential to an informed citizenry in a democracy. Tendencies in government to cover up by secrecy wrongdoing or inefficiency should be resisted by the Christian citizen. Books, such as *Going into Politics* by Robert E. Merriam and Rachel M. Goetz (Harper & Brothers, New York, 1957), are helpful manuals to one desiring to take an interest in his civic responsibilities.

Evangelical Christians will only be able to fulfill in a democracy a Christian conception of citizenship if they will study the issues involved in the development of domestic and foreign policy. They should also be acquainted with the educational, moral and spiritual qualifications of those seeking office so that they can use their franchise intelligently. Some may find they do this better as an independent voter. Others may, under the primary system in some states, register as a member of a party so that they have a voice in the choice of candidates. There is nothing to prevent ministers from discussing political issues in the light of Biblical truth and urging people to fulfill their obligations of citizenship in the light of Biblical principles.

Once officials are chosen, the Christian will watch to see that the best policies from a Christian viewpoint are followed. More Christians could write letters to their congressmen on vital issues. Organizations, such as the National Association of Evangelicals, seek through their periodicals to keep the Christian informed on issues in national and state life concerning which he may write to his representatives or join with others in the use of the petition. Where practicable, interviews with officials may do much to keep the government up to a high state of morality. The complexity of politics in the modern world is no excuse for ignorance of governmental affairs on the part of a Christian. Many excellent and generally objective sources of information are available. Possession of such information should prevent the Christian citizen from being a passive or neutral citizen. Responsibility and privilege involve the willingness to participate in common interests.

Fear of punishment should not be the only motive which leads to tax-paying (Rom. 13:5). A conscience that is clear with respect to citizenship is suggested also by the apostle. Peter suggested that constructive Christian citizenship is one of the best answers to false accusations against the moral character of Christianity (I Peter 2:15).

Every effort should be made to protect the rights even of minorities with whom we may disagree. If any are deprived of legitimate rights, such as freedom from arrest without a warrant and freedom of religion, there is nothing in time to prevent the loss of all these rights for all. Neither should minorities, misusing these rights in the name of religious freedom or freedom of speech, be allowed to deprive others of these rights. Any minority, whether economic, religious or political, which seeks to dominate the state, should meet with opposition from the Christian citizen.

Scientific and technological advances in the art of war and man's depraved nature make the destruction of civilization in war a possibility. Hence, the Christian will be interested in the elimination of war as a factor in the policies of government so far as it is practicable. It is interesting to note that the church in World War II did not sanctify the war as a Holy War as did the church in World War I. Instead the church gave its attention to providing chaplains to meet spiritual needs of men, to raising money to alleviate suffering and to aid in reconstruction after the war.

The United Nations General Assembly provides an excellent opportunity for the marshaling of world public opinion against states which violate established international law, treaties or basic principles of morality in the name of expediency. It was a committee of the United Nations which held up to the moral disapproval of the world the brutal treatment of the Hungarians by Russia. Support of the UN in this respect need not involve approval of all its activities, such as, for instance, the atheistic educational activities of UNESCO, the educational branch of the United Nations. The Evangelical will support disarmament with adequate systems of inspection necessary in a world that is still "tares and wheat." Support of international policies for pacific settlement of disputes and for the promotion of international trade should not be out of order for the Christian citizen. He desires to promote anything that will make for the economic well-being of all lands and promote better understanding of other people.

2. *Economic Responsibilities*

The Christian also should give attention to the sphere of economics. The church too long has let the worker slip out of the sphere of its influence. Only about twenty per cent of church members in the United States are members of unions. The worker and the church must be meaningfully related in Christ so that Christianity becomes relevant to his problems.

This becomes most personal in the matter of vocation. The great leaders of the Reformation, such as Luther and Calvin, upheld the idea that a Christian could be called of God to a suitable vocation whereby he could make his living and in so doing serve God and his fellows. This ended the idea of any separation between the sacred and the secular (I Tim. 4:4). Creative work is a blessing given to man in the Garden by the express command of God (Gen. 2:15) and can be dedicated to God. Only since the Fall has man had to eat his bread by the "sweat of his face" (Gen. 3:19a). He was also to devote six out of seven days to economic activity in his efforts to subdue the earth and have dominion over it (Gen. 1:28; Exod. 20:8-11).

Saints and Society in the Twentieth Century 171

These principles will keep the Christian out of economic activities which are not for the glory of God or the good of others. It is inconceivable that a Christian would engage in the production of intoxicating drinks or drugs that would harm his fellows.

Individuals as actual and potential sons of God should be objects of dignity and not exploitation. Persons are more important than things. Ideally the Christian worker in his work should be interested in the production of quality as well as quantity, although he may face the opposition of those who seek to hold down production. It is at this point that the Christian owner of assembly line plants will seek as far as possible to make work meaningful. This is difficult because the assembly line calls for only monotonously repetitive mechanical actions, which can be learned easily and which depersonalize work and the worker. Perhaps automation, which makes the machine the slave and frees the worker for work involving greater skills, may be a great help in again putting the individual to constructive and relatively creative work.

The Christian is commanded to work in order that he may be independent, self-sustaining and honest in his financial obligations to others (I Thess. 4:11, 12; II Thess. 3:12). In his acquisition of wealth he will remember that he does not own, but only administers as a steward, what God has given him, and that he is accountable to God for his stewardship of life (Deut. 8:17, 18; Acts 20:25; Luke 16:1-15, 19-31; Eph. 4:28). Wesley advised his Methodists to earn and save all they could, but then added that they should be ready to give all they could.

This same conception of the stewardship of wealth has been observed in the lives of Wilberforce and Shaftesbury. When the estates he inherited from his father needed renovating to make more livable conditions for the cottagers, Shaftesbury did not hesitate to sell treasured family portraits to get money to build model housing or to repair the parish church. Wealth used only for the possessor leads to stultification of spiritual life.

The Christian will remember that labor is not merely a commodity nor a man a thing, but that a man is worth more than property. He will support equality of economic opportunity irrespective of race, religion, sex or rank in society. Just pay for work done and fair treatment should characterize the employer, whether an individual or corporation. The problems of the relationship of labor and management or capital become important at this point. Lands, factories, bank accounts, stocks and bonds may in the eyes of the courts of law be considered as an aboslute possession except where public safety and welfare is involved, but in the sight of God they are possessions which only God absolutely owns and which the Christian possesses as a good steward. (Ps. 24:1, 2; 50:1, 2; Deut. 10:14; Hag. 2:8; Luke 12:13-21; cf. Gen. 1:26, 28; 2:15). Wealth is a means, not an end. It is something one possesses under God for leading a good life and for which one is accountable to God. Likewise the worker who is a Christian with no commodity except the skill of his hands is a steward of the abilities he has. As both capital and labor see money or property as a trust from God to be used for God's glory and the good of men, relations between the two could be put on a more spiritual basis. James' warning against the misuse of riches would then be heeded (James 1:9-11; 2:1-7; 5:1-6).

Recognition of these principles and the statements of Paul concerning capital and labor would be of value if applied to labor relations. Neither business nor labor should be allowed to hold a life and death power over one's right to work or over the price structure. Paul's advice in Ephesians 6:5-8 and Colossians 3:22-25 would seem to be an excellent code for relations between captial and labor in the economic process. Work should be service to God as well as to men. The owner

Saints and Society in the Twentieth Century 173

should pay a fair and just living wage and avoid tyrannizing his workers, because both he and the worker must remember that they are finally accountable to God. It is on such principles that the Christian Labor Association, which is recognized by the National Labor Relations Board, is organized. Fair profits and wages and no Sunday labor are some of the ideals of the organization. When men forget these things, government, through an aroused public opinion, may have to set conditions by law which should have been the voluntary rule for those who professed Christianity. Labor unions and restrictive legislation on behalf of the public welfare came because capital forgot its divine obligations. Labor, which has become an equally great monopoly, also may be forced by law, which should not be a "union-busting" device, to recognize that with privilege goes responsibility to the public interest. Such responsibility involves avoiding violence, bargaining in good faith and keeping negotiated agreements. Too often the modern union leader puts more emphasis on economic gain than the real interest of the worker. Abuse of power, whether political or, in the case of corporations and unions, economic, is a matter of concern to the Christian citizen.

Where war, crisis, famine, natural disaster, automation, the ineptness of the worker or his faulty personality may create unemployment, the Christian will be interested in meeting human need in the same manner as Christ who "went about doing good." That the relief of need was a practice of the Early Church is amply proved by the evidence in the New Testament. When the need of temporary aid to those at Jerusalem at the season of Pentecost arose, Christians, such as Barnabas, did not hesitate to sell property to meet the need of those Jews who had become Christians and who were in need of a period of instruction before they returned to their homes. This was a temporary and voluntary practice of communism to meet a special need, and was based upon the

Christian's recognition that they were stewards who possessed under God, rather than owned, their property. That the dispensing of charity to needy widows was a customary practice is evidenced in the appointment of deacons in Acts 6 and the instructions concerning the care of widows in I Timothy 5: 3-16. Some women, such as Dorcas, made garments for those who needed clothing (Acts 9:36-39). When the Church in Jerusalem was faced with a famine, the Gentile churches made a contribution to their need (Acts 11:29). Wherever there was economic need, the church was active.

Such aid given personally in a spirit of love has an advantage over our modern system of charity which many times is dispensed by professional case workers in a cold, impersonal manner, although the size of welfare loads in big cities may make the latter necessary. Such was the type of loving aid that the products of revival in eighteenth century England gave to those in need. This was true of Wesley, his followers, Wilberforce and Shaftesbury.

Perhaps the church has lost much in letting welfare pass from its sphere of action to the state. There are still, however, many areas of personal economic aid in which the church can participate. There are many evangelical brethren in many parts of the world whom evangelical Christians should be helping. At this point one cannot help but think of evangelical postwar relief or of the work of Christian agencies which have done so much for orphans and others who were needy in Korea. This is continuing the spirit of the great revivalists of the eighteenth century who tried to meet economic as well as spiritual need to the best of their ability.

In all his work to relate his faith to economic problems, the Christian will realize that the sinfulness of man, reflected in the economic order, makes a just economic order through a collectivistic welfare-state impossible. His hope of the Second Advent reassures him that a just order will one day be brought about by divine action. In the light of this hope he

Saints and Society in the Twentieth Century 175

will try to put Biblical principles to work insofar as possible in the economic order.

3. *Social Responsibilities*

The area of social problems provides another area of activity in which the Christian should participate meaningfully. The problems created by differences between races should be a matter of concern to the Christian because of his Christian conception of the church as an area in which all are brethren. Love to God is to be balanced by love to one's neighbors. Although Paul was a rabid Jew, when he became a Christian, he became conscious of his obligation to Gentiles as well as Jews. He acknowledged himself to be debtor to "Greeks and Barbarians" (Rom. 1:14-16). He reminded the Colossians (3:11) that in Christ there was no room for distinctions based upon race, and it is apparent from Acts that he carried out this principle in his own life. It is sad that more progress seems to have been made in desegregation in sports and the armed forces than in the church, which should offer fellowship to all fellow-believers.

The church through its leadership should inform its people as to what is the Biblical teaching and practice that should guide the individual Christian in his relationship with those of other races. Paul believed that all were "made out of one" (Acts 17:26), that God is no respecter of persons (Acts 10:34, 35) and that by faith in Christ, race distinctions are wiped out (Gal. 3:28). The Christian will never be a party in the economic sphere to economic discrimination which puts a job opening on a basis of the proper color of skin rather than upon ability. He will insist upon equality of economic as well as political opportunity. Because of the long period in which racial prejudices have been built up in the United States and South Africa and the tensions in Asia and Africa created by imperialism, the Christian will endeavor to be patient in dealing with others in seeking to bring about a recognition of equality in the political and economic spheres.

This will involve, in this writer's opinion, neither forced integration nor segregation but a developing pluralistic society which is the genius of a democracy. The problem of social relations will soon solve themselves if political and economic opportunity are accorded. People of other races who continue to exist as cultural and social groups may have much to enrich our culture.

In any event, Biblical principles, rather than age-old prejudices, should mark the treatment which Christians accord to those of other races. Perhaps if the Church in Germany had been more aware of personalizing the gospel in the area of race relations, the horrible fate which befell the Jews might have been avoided, and the Germans, instead of making atonement now by grants of money to Israel, might have been profiting through peaceful international trade through the efforts of these able people. Christians have much work to do in almost every land to understand the teaching of Scripture on this matter and then, as individuals, to make a practical application of it in their lives.

Gambling, vice and the sale of narcotics are other sins to which our society too often has closed its eyes. The Church should certainly make its followers aware that Christ's standard is single and similar for both men and women in the area of sex relationships, so that Christians will apply it in their own lives and seek to help others who have problems in this area. Publishers of obscene magazines could be made to face hostile public pressure created by Christians, who band together with others of like mind on this point, so that such publishers, because of public disapproval, shall be brought to abandon the publication of such literature. Certainly the present success of the campaign against pornography is a case in point.

Disclosures in recent years have alerted those, who have

Saints and Society in the Twentieth Century 177

given the matter any consideration, to the problem of the treatment of those suffering from mental disease. It has been demonstrated in several cases that many, who in past time would be kept in a mental hospital for life, are helped back to reality by trained personnel or can be cured with drugs. This may demand the allocation of more tax monies temporarily, but, if more people can be returned to society to become useful productive members of society, it will be cheaper and certainly more Christian in the long run. The Christian citizen should be interested in such problems to the point where he becomes informed and willing to promote action favorable to the end of restoring the maximum number to society and to Christ.

That conditions in prisons are not idyllic even in our modern society is evidenced by prison riots and attempts at mass breaks. The early Evangelicals took time to visit prisoners and to give them food, clothes and the Word of God. The need of food and clothes may not be so great in our society, which provides such for prisoners, but there are many areas where advance may be made to the end that many might again become useful members of society. A few evangelical Christians, through prison chaplaincies and through aid to released prisoners, are endeavoring to put the Gospel into practice, but more need to become interested, informed and active in this area in order that our whole prison system might be overhauled in the light of Christian principles.

The Christian ought to attack problems in all the spheres which have been discussed in the light of what is the Biblical teaching on the matter. This will involve action in dealing with such problems by co-operation with those of like mind. It is difficult, if not impossible, to demonstrate Biblically that the church, as an organization, should participate as a pressure group in the social order. This study shows that the success achieved by Wilberforce came because informed Christians with integrity joined with other Christians, and even with those who were not Christians, in order to achieve common ends for the good of men. Co-operation in a common good end does not involve compromise when one limits the co-operation to a common end. Bentham had little use for Wilberforce's principles, and Wilberforce for his, but they worked together to free the slave.

The Christian will endeavor to have as few blind spots as possible in dealing with problems which arise from participation in the economic or political life of his day. Buxton, in his day, apparently saw no conflict between the fact that he made his money in a brewery, whose product surely brought strife and economic hardship into many English homes, and his advocacy of the freedom of the slaves within the British Empire. Shaftesbury, who was a real benefactor of the English working man, could not see fit to support any movement to grant the franchise to the English working men. We should not, in dealing with the mote in another's eye, be oblivious to the beam in our own eye.

Contemporary Evangelicals, who for a time ignored their responsibility as Christians in society, are becoming increasingly aware that, while the first function of the Christian is to preach the Gospel in order to win others to Christ, they also have a responsibility to put the principles of Christ into action in individual lives as well as in co-operation with others in the social order in which they live. If they follow Paul's principle (Gal. 6:10) they will first meet the needs of fellow believers in whatever areas are necessary and then engage in a wider discharge of their duty to "do good to all men." Application of their faith in loving service will be characterized neither by pessimism, which paralyzes action because of its belief that the world is doomed anyway and nothing can be done, nor by a Utopianism which misleads them into thinking that Christians can create a perfect world. Instead, with the coming of Christ in mind as the final and permanent answer to the world's problems, they will occupy faithfully and fully both by preaching the Gospel to the lost and by applying the Gospel to the needs of society. No political, economic or social order will be ideal or final until Christ Himself destroys sin and its author.

Conditions in our twentieth century world differ only in degree, not in kind, from those of needy eighteenth century England. These godly men, whose scope of activity and spirit of action have been examined, did not let the problems daunt them. As Christians, they faced their social order with the light of the Gospel. This created a sensitive conscience which made these Christians salt. The modern Christian is to walk humbly before God, but he is also to deal justly and to love mercy (Micah 6:8). We should not forget also that we were saved "unto good works" (Eph. 2:10) as well as to witness. Paul urged that those who believed should be "careful to maintain good works" (Titus 3:8). This keynote is struck again and again in the New Testament. While we should be sure our social theory is genuinely Biblical and Christian, we should when enlightened as to our responsibility, which enlightening is the task of the pastor, proceed to act as Christian citizens for the glory of God and for the good of men so as to "occupy" faithfully until our Lord's return (I Thess. 1:3; cf. 9, 10). Is our faith sufficient and our love deep enough to bring us to the point of action while we hopefully await His imminent return? Christ can transform in history as well as beyond history. Revival should, as it has in the past, result in service to society as well as the salvation of souls.

BIBLIOGRAPHY

I. SOURCE BOOKS

Buxton, Charles, ed., *Memoirs of Sir Thomas Fowell Buxton, Bart.* (London: John Murray, 2nd. ed., 1849)

Campbell, John, *Travels in South Africa* (London: Francis Westley, 2 vols., 1822)

Chamberlin, David, *Some Letters from Livingstone, 1840-1877* (London: Oxford University Press, 1940)

Curnock, Nehemiah, ed., *The Journal of the Rev. John Wesley* (London: The Epworth Press, 8 vols., 1938)

Hodder, Edwin, *The Life and Work of the Seventh Earl of Shaftesbury, K. G.* (London: Cassell & Co., Ltd., 3 vols., 1888)

Krapf, J. Lewis, *Travels, Researches, and Missionary Labors During an Eighteen-Year Residence in East Africa* (London: Trübner & Co., 1860)

Livingstone, David, *Missionary Travels and Researches in South Africa* (New York: Harper & Brothers, 1868)

Livingstone, David, and Livingstone, Charles, *Narrative of an Expedition to the Zambezi and Its Tributaries . . .* (New York: Harper & Brothers, 1866)

Livingstone, David, *The Last Journals of David Livingstone . . .* (New York: Harper & Brothers, 1875)

Mackenzie, John, *Austral-Africa, Losing It or Ruling It* (London: Low, Marston, Searle & Rivington, 2 vols., 1887)

Moffatt, Robert, *Missionary Labors and Scenes in South Africa* (London: John Snow, 1842)

Moir, W., *After Livingstone* (London: Hodder & Stoughton, 3rd. ed., 1924)

Philip, John, *Researches in South Africa* (London: James Duncan, 1828)

Report from the Select Committee on Aborigines (London: Parliamentary Paper No. 538, 1836)

182   *Saints and Society*

Report from the Select Committee on Aborigines (London: Parliamentary Paper No. 425, 1837)

Stanley, Henry M., *How I Found Livingstone* (New York: Scribner, Armstrong & Co., 1872)

Telford, John, ed., *The Letters of the Rev. John Wesley* (London: The Epworth Press, 8 vols., 1931)

Tucker, Alfred R., *Eighteen Years in Uganda and East Africa* (London: Edward Arnold, 2 vols., 1908)

Wilberforce, A. M., *The Private Papers of William Wilberforce* (London: T. Fisher Union, 1897)

Wilberforce, Robert I., and Wilberforce, Samuel, eds., *The correspondence of William Wilberforce* (London, 2 vols. 1848). Published by the editors.

Wilberforce, William, *A Practical View* . . . (Philadelphia: Key & Biddle, 1835)

Young, E. D., *Nyasa—A Journal of Adventures* (London: John Murray, 2nd. ed. rev. by Horace Waller, 1877)

II. SECONDARY BOOKS SOME OF WHICH CONTAIN MUCH PRIMARY MATERIAL

Balleine, G. R., *A History of the Evangelical Party in the Church of England* (New York: Longmans, Green and Co., 1911)

Belden, Albert D., *George Whitefield, The Awakener* (New York: The Macmillan Company, 2nd. rev. ed., 1953)

Bennett, John, *The Christian as Citizen* (New York: Association Press, 1955)

Blaikie, William G., *The Personal Life of David Livingstone* (New York, Laymen's Missionary Movement, 1880)

Although marked by hero worship, this book contains data from sources which later biographers were unable to obtain.

Booth, Charles, *Zachary Macaulay* (New York: Longmans, Green and Co., 1934)

Bready, John W., *England: Before and After Wesley* (New York: Harper & Brothers, 1938)

———, *Lord Shaftesbury and Social-Industrial Progress* (London: George Allen and Unwin, Ltd., 1926)

Bibliography

———, *Wesley and Democracy* (Toronto: The Ryerson Press, 1939)

Campbell, Reginald J., *Livingstone* (New York: Dodd, Mead and Company, 1930)
This biography is more objective than that of Blaikie.

Carrington, Charles E., *The British Overseas* (Cambridge: The University Press, 1950)

Carter, Henry, *The Methodist Heritage* (London: The Epworth Press, 2nd. ed., 1951)

Church, Leslie F., *More About the Early Methodist People* (London: The Epworth Press, 1949)

Coupland, Reginald, *The British Anti-Slavery Movement* (London: Thornton Butterworth Ltd., 1933)

———, *Wilberforce, a Narrative* (Oxford: Clarendon Press, 1923)
This is a sympathetic yet objective biography of Wilberforce.

Cowherd, Raymond G., *The Politics of English Dissent* (New York: New York University Press, 1956)

DeBoer, Cecil, *Responsible Protestantism* (Grand Rapids: Wm. B. Eerdmans Publishing Co., 1957)

Dennis, James S., *Christian Missions and Social Progress* (Westwood, N. J.: Fleming H. Revell Co., 3 vols., 1897-1906)

Edwards, Maldwyn, *John Wesley and the Eighteenth Century* (New York: The Abingdon Press, 1933)

Elliot-Binns, Leonard E., *The Early Evangelicals* (London: Lutterworth Press, 1953)

Green, J. E. S., *Rhodes Goes North* (London: G. Bell and Sons, Ltd., 1936)

Griggs, Earl L., *Thomas Clarkson, the Friend of Slaves* (London: George Allen & Unwin Ltd., 1936)

Groves, Charles P., *The Planting of Christianity in Africa* (London: Lutterworth Press, 4 vols., 1948-1958)

Halévy, Elié, *A History of the English People in 1815*, trans. by Edward I. Watkin and D. A. Barker (New York: Harcourt, Brace and Company, 1924)

Hammond, John L., and Hammond, Barbara, *Lord Shaftesbury* (London: Constable & Co., Ltd., 1923)
The Hammonds have little appreciation of the religious motivation of his work.
Harding, Frederick A. J., *The Social Impact of the Evangelical Revival* (London: The Epworth Press, 1947)
Harris, J. H., *The Story of Robert Raikes for the Young* (Philadelphia: The Union Press, 1900)
Harris, John, *A Century of Emancipation* (London: J. M. Dent & Sons, 1953)
Hawker, George, *The Life of George Grenfell, Congo Missionary and Explorer* (Westwood, N. J.: Fleming H. Revell, 2nd. ed., 1909)
Henry, Stuart C., *George Whitefield, Wayfaring Witness* (New York: Abingdon Press, 1957)
Hodder, Edwin, *The Seventh Earl of Shaftesbury, K. G., as Social Reformer* (Westwood, N. J.: Fleming H. Revell Co., 1898)
Howse, Ernest, *Saints in Politics* (Toronto: The University of Toronto Press, 1952)
This is a fine survey of the work of the Clapham Sect.
Johnston, Harry H., *George Grenfell and the Congo* (London: Hutchinson & Co., 2 vols., 1908)
———, *Livingstone and the Exploration of Central Africa* (London: George Philip and Son, 1891)
———, *The Uganda Protectorate* (London: Hutchinson & Co., 2 vols., 1902)
Klingberg, Frank J., *The Anti-Slavery Movement in England* (New Haven: Yale University Press, 1926)
Knutsford, Viscountess, *Life and Letters of Zachary Macaulay* (London: Edward Arnold, 1900)
Lascelles, Edward C. P., *Granville Sharp and the Freedom of Slaves in England* (London: Oxford University Press, 1928)
Letts, Harold C., ed., *Christian Social Responsibility* (Philadelphia: Muhlenberg Press, 3 vols., 1957)
This approach is congenial to the evangelical outlook.
Loane, Marcus L., *Cambridge and the Evangelical Succession* (London: Lutterworth Press, 1952)

———, *Oxford and the Evangelical Succession* (London: Lutterworth Press, 1950)

Lovett, Richard, *The History of the London Missionary Society 1795-1895* (London: Oxford University Press, 2 vols., 1899)

Lugard, Frederick A., *The Story of the Uganda Protectorate* (London: H. Marshall & Son, 1900)

Mackenzie, W. Douglas, *John Mackenzie, South African Missionary and Statesman* (London: Hodder & Stoughton, 1902)

Macmillan, William M., *Bantu, Boer and Briton* (London: Faber and Gweyer, 1929)

———, *The Cape Color Question* (London: Faber and Gweyer, 1927)

Martin, K. L. P., *Missionaries and Annexation in the Pacific* (Oxford: Oxford University Press, 1924)

Maston, T. B., *Christianity and World Issues* (New York: The Macmillan Company, 1957)

Maston's approach is quite sympathetic to an evangelical viewpoint, and his suggestions are practical rather than idealistic.

Mathieson, William L., *British Slavery and Its Abolition 1823-1828* (London: Longmans, Green and Co., 1926)

———, *British Slave Emancipation 1839-1849* (London: Longmans, Green and Co., 1932)

———, *Great Britain and the Slave Trade, 1839-1865* (London: Longmans, Green and Co., 1929)

Moffat, John S., *The Lives of Robert and Mary Moffat* (New York: Armstrong, 1886)

Newton, Arthur P., *A Hundred Years of the British Empire* (New York: The Macmillan Company, 1940)

Nicolson, Harold G., *The Congress of Vienna* (New York: Harcourt, Brace, and Co., 1946)

Niebuhr, H. Richard, *Christ and Culture* (New York: Harper & Brothers, 1951)

Obenhaus, Victor, *The Responsible Christian* (Chicago: The University of Chicago Press, 1957)

Ogilivie, James N., *Our Empire's Debt to Missions* (London: Hodder & Stoughton, 1924)

Oswell, W. Edward, *William Cotton Oswell, Hunter and Explorer* (London: William Heinemann, 2 vols., 1900)

Rasmussen, Albert T., *Christian Social Ethics* (Englewood Cliffs, N. J.: Prentice-Hall, Inc., 1956)

Rattenbury, J. Ernest, *Wesley's Legacy to the World* (Nashville: Cokesbury Press, 1929)

Seaver, George, *David Livingstone: His Life and Letters* (New York: Harper & Brothers, 1957)

A recent biography based upon newer sources and sympathetic to Livingstone.

Snyder, Louis L., *The Age of Reason* (New York: D. Van Nostrand Company, Inc., 1955)

Spann, J. Richard L., *The Church and Social Responsibility* (Nashville: Abingdon-Cokesbury Press, 1953)

Stead, Francis H., *The Story of Social Christianity* (London: James Clarke & Co., Limited, 2 vols., n.d.)

Stephen, James, *Essays in Ecclesiastical Biography* (London: Longmans, Green and Co., 2 vols., 1907)

Stephen, Leslie, and Lee, Sidney, eds., *Dictionary of National Biography* (Oxford: Oxford University Press, 22 vols., 1937-1938)

Stewart, James, *Lovedale, South Africa* (Edinburgh: Andrew Elliot, 1894)

Stock, Eugene, *The History of the Church Missionary Society* (London: Church Missionary Society, 2 vols., 1899-1916)

Stock, Sarah G., *The Story of Uganda and the Victoria-Nyanza Mission* (Westwood, N. J.: Fleming H. Revell Company, 1892)

Tenney, Mary Alice, *Blueprint for a Christian World* (Winona Lake, Ind.: Light and Life Press, 1953)

Tyerman, Luke, *The Life and Times of the Rev. John Wesley* (London: Hodder and Stoughton, 6th. ed., 3 vols., 1890)

Walker, Eric A., *A History of South Africa* (London: Longmans, Green and Co., 1924)

Wearmouth, Robert F., *Methodism and the Working-class Movements of England 1800-1850* (London: The Epworth Press, 1947)

Wilberforce, Robert I., and Wilberforce, Samuel, *The Life of William Wilberforce,* abridged by Caspar Morris (Philadelphia: Henry Perkins, 1839)

III. UNPUBLISHED MATERIAL

Cairns, Earle E., "The Political and Humanitarian Activities of the London Missionary Society in South Africa, 1799-1857," Ph.D. Dissertation (Lincoln: University of Nebraska, 1941)

Cairns, Earle E., "The Role of British Missionaries in the History of Central and South Africa 1800-1900," M.A. Thesis (Lincoln: University of Nebraska, 1939)

Loveless, Robert C., "The Teachings of Jesus With Relation to the Social Program of the Church," M.A. Thesis (Wheaton, Ill.: Wheaton College, 1948)

Wiens, John, "Biblical Roots of Evangelical Reform Movements in England, 1729-1885," M.A. Thesis (Wheaton, Ill.: Wheaton College, 1958)

INDEX

Aborigines Committee, 86-87
Aborigines Protection Society, 86-87, 91
Aborigines Report, 91
Addington, 70
African Association, 71
African Institution, 74, 77, 78
African Lakes Company, 55, 93, 99
Agency Committee, 83, 151
Alexander I, of Russia, 75
Anabaptists, 165
Anti-Slavery and Aborigines Protection Society, 87
Anti-Slavery Reporter, 79, 81, 153
Anti-Slavery Committee, 71
Anti-Slavery Society, 59, 79, 81
A Practical View . . ., 73, 125-128

Babington, Thomas, 49, 76, 124
Bacon, Francis, 24
Ball, Hannah, 103
Barnabas, 173
Bechuanaland, 97-99
Bedford, Duke of, 20
Benezet, Anthony, 58
Bentham, Jeremy, 142, 154, 178
Bentinck, William, 82
Bible, Shaftesbury's view, 128-129; Evangelicals' view, 140-141
Blackstone, William, 27, 62
Blantyre Mission, 54
Boers, 95, 97-99
Böhler, Peter, 121
Brenton, 88
British and Foreign Anti-Slavery Society, 87
British and Foreign Bible Society, 48-49, 129
British East India Company, 49-50, 141, 154, 161
Browning, Elizabeth Barrett, 152
Buchanan, Consul, 100
Buchanan, John, 93

Bull, G .S., 113, 114
Burton, John, 121
Buxton, T. Fowell, 41, 57, 77, 78, 79-87, 88, 89, 90-91, 95, 107, 108, 150, 151, 154, 178

Caddell, 125
Camden, Lord, 69
Campbell, John, 51
Carey, William, 45
Caroline, 19
Castlereagh, Lord, 75
Charles, Thomas, 48
Chesterfield, Lord, 19-20
Chimney sweeps, 117
Christian Labor Association, 173
Churchmen's Commission for Decent Publications, 159
Christian Observer, 73, 78, 152
Church and society, 160-162
Church Missionary Society, 41, 46-47, 95, 101
Clapham Sect, 39-42, 71, 74, 76, 78
Clarkson, Thomas, 40, 41, 58, 59, 63, 65, 66-68, 70, 71, 72, 77, 82, 149, 150, 152, 153
Coke, Thomas, 35
Colenso, Bishop, 129
Collingwood, Luke, 64
Committee on the treatment of aborigines, 86-87
Communism, 135-136, 163
Condorcet, 24
Cooper, Anthony Ashley; see Shaftesbury
Cowper, Lady Emily, 111
Cowper, William, 38, 72, 152

Davies, Samuel, 105
Deism, 26, 29
Descartes, 24
Dickson, 72
Djilas, Milovan, 136

189

190   Saints and Society

Doddridge, Philip, 70, 124
Dolben, Sir William, 71
Dorcas, 174
Drunkenness in eighteenth century England, 22-23
Duncan, John, 93
Dundas, 73
D'Urban, Governor, 94

Economic order, and the Christian, 170-175
Edwards, Jonathan, 141
Emancipation Act of 1833, 83-84
Engels, Friedrich, 135
England, conditions during eighteenth century, 17-28
Erhardt, 51, 52
Evangelical Welfare Agency, 159
Exeter Hall, 42, 48, 90, 101, 152, 153
Exploration by missionaries, 51-55
Eyre, John, 45, 46

Factory acts, 115-116
Faith, Wesley's view, 122; Wilberforce's view, 124; Shaftesbury's view, 130; Evangelical view, 140-143
Family, functions, 156-157; problems, 157-158; Christian responsibility to, 158-159
Fascism, 163
Fielden, 115
Finney, Charles, 141
Fletcher, John, 38
Fosdick, Harry Emerson, 143
Fox, George, 58
Fry, Elizabeth, 79, 80, 107-108
Funnell, Thomas, 59

Gambling in eighteenth century England, 23
George III, 19, 27
George IV, 19
Gisbourne, 49, 74
Gladstone, William E., 160
Glasgow Missionary Society, 46
Gordon, Robert, 110
Graham, Billy, 141
Grant, Charles, 40, 48, 49, 50-51

Grellet Stephen, 107
Grenfell, George, 51, 54
Grimshaw, William, 37
Griquas, 94
Gurney, Priscilla, 80
Gutzlaff, Charles, 52

Haweis, 45
Hawkins, John, 56
Herbert of Cherbury, 26
Hoare, Samuel, 59
Hobson, William, 96
Hodder, Edwin, 128, 131
Holy Club, 31, 34, 103, 121
Hopkey, Sophia, 34
Horne, Melville, 45
Hottentots, 88-90
Howard, John, 36, 106-107
Hughes, Joseph, 48
Huntingdon, Countess of, 32, 33

Imperial British East Africa Company, 101
Insane, treatment, and reform, 110; Christian and, 177

Jackson, Thomas, 150, 151

Kaffirs, 95
Kent, Duke of, 19
Kerr, James, 62
Kok, Adam, 94
Krapf, 51, 52

Labor, the Christian and, 172-173
Laird, Captain, 62
Lisle, David, 62
Livingstone, David, 46, 51, 52-54, 91-93, 99
Livingstonia Central African Trading Company, 93; see African Lakes Company
Livingstonia Mission, 54
Locke, John, 18, 24
London Missionary Society, 45-46, 88, 152
Love to God and man, Wesley's view, 122-123; Shaftesbury's view, 130-131; Evangelical view, 143-146
Luther, Martin, 138

Macaulay, Zachary, 40-41, 49, 65, 73, 74, 77-79, 81, 82, 83, 89, 120, 150, 152
Mackay, Alexander, 55
Mackenzie, John, 46, 97-99
Mackinnon, William, 101
Manning, William, 125
Mansfield, Lord, 62-63
Marsden, Samuel, 95-96
Martyn, Henry, 47, 51
Marx, Karl, 135, 136, 145, 147
Mauritius scandal, 82
Mercantilism, 20-21
Middleton, Charles and Lady, 70
Mill, John Stuart, 142
Millis, Maria, 109, 130
Mills, Selina, 78
Milner, Isaac, 37, 39, 69, 70, 124
Mines Act, 116-117
Minorities, the Christian and, 169
Mirabeau, 67
Missionary Travels and Researches in South Africa, 92
Missionary societies, organization of, 45-48
Moffat, Mary, 53
Moffat, Robert, 46, 52, 97
Montanists, 146
Montanus, 134
Moody, Dwight, 141
More, Hannah, 41, 104
Mormons, 165
Münster, 165
Mutesa, 100
Mwanga, 100, 101

National Association of Evangelicals, 158, 161, 168
Nazism, 163
Nero, 162
Newton, Isaac, 24
Newton, John, 36, 38, 70, 124
New Zealand, 47, 95-97
Nightingale, Florence, 117-118
Nyasaland, 99-100

Oastler, Richard, 111-112
Observance of Sunday, 161
Ordinance Fifty, 89

Parker, Isaac, 149
Peel, Robert, 111, 115
Perceval, 49, 70
Philip, John, 46, 86, 87-90, 94-95, 152
Pinto, Serpa, 100
Pitt, William, 39, 41, 69, 71, 73, 125
Pope, Alexander, 25
Portal, Gerald, 101
Potter, John, 27
Pratt, Josiah, 80
Preaching in eighteenth century, 27
Prisoners, Christian and, 177
Proclamation Society, 70

Race relations, the Christian and, 175-176
Ragged Schools, 105
Raikes, Robert, 103
Ramsay, James, 64, 66-67, 70
Rauschenbusch, Walter, 136-138, 142
Rebmann, 51, 52
Researches in South Africa, 89
Rhodes, Cecil, 93, 97-98
Road builders, missionary, 55
Romaine, William, 33, 37
Rousseau, Jean, 18, 24

Sadler, Michael, 112-113
Salisbury, Prime Minister, 100
Second Coming of Christ, Wilberforce on, 125; Shaftesbury on, 131-132, 134; Evangelicals and, 146-148, 174-175
Sex, Christian and, 176
Shaftesbury, 21, 30, 98, 102, 104, 105, 108-118, 120, 121; theology of social action, 128-132, 134, 147, 150-151, 161-162, 171, 174, 178
See Cooper, Anthony Ashley
Sharp, Granville, 40, 48, 59, 61-66, 121, 149, 152
Shore, John, 40, 48-49
Sierra Leone, 64-65, 78, 83, 150
Simeon, Charles, 37, 39
Slavery, Quaker opposition, 58; Methodist opposition, 58-60; abolition in England, 61-63; abolition in British Empire, 84-85

Slave trade, Arab, 53, 92; English, 56-58; abolition in England, 66-74; Denmark, 75; France, 75; Holland, 75; Portugal, 75-76; Spain, 76; Sweden, 75; United States, 75; at Congress of Vienna, 75; suppression by naval patrols, 74, 90; by commerce, 90-94; amelioration in British Empire, 76-77
Smeathman, Henry, 64
Smith, Adam, 21, 24, 29
Smith, William, 81
Social Gospel, 133, 136-138
Society for the Abolition of the Slave Trade, 67
Society for the Extinction of the Slave Trade and the Civilization of Africa, 90
Society for the Reformation of Prison Discipline, 80
Society for the Suppression of Vice, 70
Somersett, James, 63
Spangenberg, August, 121
Spengler, Oswald, 146
Stanley, 100
State, responsibility of, 163-166; its function, 166; obligations of Christian to, 166-169; Christ and, 165; Peter and, 165; Paul and, 167; Christian motives to obey, 169
Stephen, George, 83, 151
Stephen, Jr., James, 42, 76, 84, 87, 96
Stephen, Sr., James, 40
Stevenson, James, 55, 93
Stewart, James, 55, 93
Stockdale, Captain, 61
Strong, Jonathan, 62
Sturge, Joseph, 85
Sunday schools, 103-104
Suppression of slave trade by naval patrols, 74, 90; by commerce, 90-94
Suttee, 82
Swift, Jonathan, 25

Tarleton, Colonel, 57
Tennent, Gilbert, 105
Tertullian, 134, 146

The African Slave Trade and Its Remedy, 90
Thornton, Henry, 39-40, 41, 49, 65, 74, 104
Thornton, John, 38
Treaty states, 94-96, 98
Tucker, Bishop, 101

Uganda, 47, 100-101
United Nations, the Christian and, 169-170
Universities Mission, 54, 99

Venn, Henry, 37, 91, 125
Venn, John, 36, 37, 41, 46, 47
Vienna, Congress of, 74-75, 153
Vocation, 170-171

Waitangi, Treaty of, 96
Walpole, Robert, 20, 23
War, the Christian and, 169, 170
Warren, General, 98
Waterboer, 94
Wealth, Christian view of, 171, 172, 174
Wedgwood, Josiah, 68, 72, 152
Wesleyan Missionary Society, 47
Wesley, Charles, 31, 32, 33, 34, 60
Wesley, John, 31, 32, 33-36, 58-60, 72, 103, 104, 106; theology of social action, 121-123, 132, 141, 143, 153, 171, 174
Whitefield, George, 30-33, 103, 105, 121, 141
Wilberforce, William, 21, 30, 36, 41, 46, 48, 49, 50, 57, 60, 65, 67, 68-76, 77, 80-81, 83, 84, 88, 89, 104, 108, 111, 113, 121; theology of social action, 123-128, 132, 149, 150, 152, 153, 154, 159, 161, 171, 174, 177, 178
Wilks, Matthew, 46
Willoughby, Henry, 61
Williams, Henry, 96
Wood, John, 112, 113

Yarmouth, Lady, 27
York, Duke of, 19

Zong, 64

www.ingramcontent.com/pod-product-compliance
Lightning Source LLC
Chambersburg PA
CBHW071423160426
43195CB00013B/1787